P9-DTP-945

Marilyn Monroe

Unseen Archives

Marilyn Monroe

Unseen Archives

Marie Clayton

p

This is a Parragon Publishing Book
First published in 2003

Parragon Publishing
Queen Street House
4 Queen Street
Bath
BA1 1HE, UK

Text ©Parragon
For details of photographs see pages 382-383

Produced by Atlantic Publishing
Designed by John Dunne

ISBN 1 40541 340 9

Printed in China

Contents

Introduction

Even many years after her death, Marilyn Monroe is still one of the greatest legends of the twentieth century. In her movies she projected a unique and fascinating persona - a child-woman who was both innocent and full of sexuality, someone whom men desired, but who women found unthreatening. In real life, she was a beautiful and complex woman who felt deeply insecure, and who just wanted to be loved enough to wipe out her unhappy past.

She was born on the wrong side of the tracks, an illegitimate and unwanted child, who spent most of her early years in a series of foster homes, and became a teenage bride rather than return to the orphanage. A few years later she discovered the one lover who would never let her down, and started an all-consuming affair with the camera. She fought every adversity and setback with determination and humor, and went on to become the most famous movie star of the twentieth century. In her brief career she appeared in several classic movies, as well as many more that are memorable only for her presence.

Marilyn Monroe: Unseen Archives charts Marilyn's fascinating life, from her unhappy childhood, through her time as a superstar, to her tragic early death. The exciting collection of photographs not only includes movie stills and portraits, but also many other less well known pictures taken during her career. The photographs are accompanied by detailed and perceptive captions, which give a rounded portrait of one of the world's greatest movie stars. Marilyn Monroe the person may no longer be with us, but Marilyn Monroe the star is an extraordinary and unforgettable woman whose legend lives on.

Acknowledgements

This book is dedicated to William and Emily Clayton.

The book would not have been possible without the help of
Jonathan Hamston, Matt Smithson, Giovanni D'Angelico, Maria Lopez-Duran,
Zohir Naciri and Scott Kirkham.

Thanks also to Kate Truman, Cliff Salter and Trevor Bunting.

Marilyn Monroe

Unseen Archives

CHAPTER ONE
Ladies of the Chorus

After Marilyn Monroe became famous, she told so many different stories about her childhood that it is often not clear where the truth lies. However, she was definitely born on 1 June 1926 in Los Angeles, just a few miles from Hollywood. Her mother, Gladys Pearl, was a film cutter, who worked at Consolidated Film Industries. Gladys had first been married to John Baker, with whom she had two children, Jack and Berniece, but the marriage had ended in divorce in 1923. Afterwards John Baker took the children back to Kentucky, leaving Gladys in California. She wasn't alone for long - in 1924 she met and married Martin Edward Mortensen. This marriage also failed, and Mortensen had long vanished from the scene before Gladys became pregnant with her third child. She never stated who the father was - perhaps she didn't really know - but one of the most likely candidates was Charles Stanley Gifford, foreman of the day shift at Consolidated. Despite this, the new baby was registered as Norma Jeane Mortensen - although during her childhood she was also sometimes known as Norma Jean Baker.

By all accounts, Gladys was not cut out to be a mother. She was still only a teenager when she gave birth to her first two children, and she had often left them with neighbors while she went out to enjoy herself. She was only just 24 when Norma Jeane was born, and was not in a settled relationship. Gladys's mother, Della Monroe, was not willing to offer help or a home, since she was about to leave on a trip round South East Asia with her current beau. Gladys had to manage on her own, with only the help of her close friend, Grace McKee. Not long after the birth she had to return to work to support herself, so she arranged for the baby to be cared for by the Bolender family, who were neighbors of Della, now back from the Far East.

Ida Bolender and her husband, Albert Wayne, were a devoutly religious couple, who looked after various local children as an extra source of income. Although Marilyn later portrayed herself as being unhappy and living in grinding poverty at this time, there is no evidence that her life was really like that. The Bolenders may not have been rich, but they lived comfortably and Norma Jeane was well dressed, had toys to play with and was not neglected. The family even owned a Model A Ford, and Norma Jeane had a pet dog named Tippy. She stayed with the Bolenders for seven years - which was the longest period of stability in her childhood. Nevertheless, it was a confusing situation for a young child - she was neither a temporary visitor, nor a part of the family. Ida Bolender had her own son, and there was a procession of other foster children, none of whom stayed as long as Norma Jeane. She later recalled having once called Ida "Mama", and being told that Ida was not her mother - the lady with the red hair was. Her mother came to visit on weekends, although these visits became less frequent as time went by. Marilyn later said that Gladys never seemed to smile, or offer any affection, so she found it difficult to think of her as "mother".

At the age of seven, Norma Jeane's world changed completely. When a neighbor killed her pet dog she was distraught with grief, and the Bolenders called Gladys. After helping to bury Tippy, Gladys paid the Bolenders to

date and took Norma Jeane away with her. She took out a mortgage on a small house in Arbol Street, near the Hollywood Bowl. To finance the payments, she let the house to an English couple with a grown-up daughter, while renting back a room for herself and Norma Jeane to live in. The couple were actors, and their daughter often worked as a stand-in. Since Gladys, and her close friend Grace McKee, were both still working at Consolidated, the talk at home was naturally full of movies and movie stars.

Unfortunately, this interlude did not last long. Early the following year Gladys was taken to hospital, having suffered a severe bout of depression that swiftly descended into some kind of mental breakdown. She was formally pronounced insane at the end of 1934, and was to spend most of her life in various hospitals until 1967,

seemingly having lost her ability to cope with normal day-to-day life for any length of time. Meanwhile, the young Norma Jeane was taken in hand by her mother's friend, Grace. Grace had no children of her own and she apparently came to regard the child almost as her own daughter, particularly after she later became Norma Jeane's legal guardian. Grace was a big fan of Jean Harlow, and she began to instil the belief that one day Norma Jeane would also be a famous movie star. She dressed the child up, showed her how to use makeup and took her to the movies regularly. However, her plans were interrupted when she met Erwin "Doc" Goddard, and he and Grace married after a whirlwind courtship. One month later, Norma Jeane entered an orphanage - perhaps because the newly married couple wanted some privacy, or because money was short and she was one mouth too many to feed. Whatever the reason, yet again Norma Jeane felt let down, unloved and abandoned - feelings that were beginning to shape how she would behave and react in the future.

The orphanage was not as bad as she later sometimes painted it, and the studio publicity machine, anxious to take advantage of any opportunity to publicize their new star, also exaggerated its supposed horrors. Grace came to take her for outings on weekends, when they went to the movies or she treated the child to a makeover at the beauty parlor.

When she left the orphanage, soon after her eleventh birthday, Norma Jeane was placed with a series of foster families, before finally going to live with Grace and her husband. Doc had three children from a previous marriage; one of them, Eleanor - known as Beebe - was around the same age as Norma Jeane and the two of them became great friends. Beebe had had a terrible childhood before this time, coping with a genuinely psychotic mother and a series of abusive foster homes, as well as grinding poverty. Many people believe that Marilyn used some of Beebe's experiences to create the story of her own abused childhood.

Once more, however, this promised stability was interrupted, when Doc was offered a job on the East Coast. Again, Norma Jeane found herself surplus to requirements, as the Goddards decided that they could not afford to take her with them. It also meant that she would lose her first real friend of her own age. However, Grace had a solution - Norma Jean should marry James, the twenty-year-old son of her friend and neighbor, Ethel Dougherty.

Although Norma Jeane and James Dougherty knew each other well, and had even dated on occasion, he was five years older than her and regarded her as still very much a child. But she had a crush on him, and he was flattered by the attention. Grace and Ethel conspired to send them out on regular dates, and soon he came to

regard Norma Jeane in a rather different light. However, they probably would not have married - except that for Norma Jeane it was marriage, or return to the orphanage, while Jim could see no real reason not to go along with the idea.

After their wedding, the young couple moved into an apartment. Norma Jeane tried hard to be a good wife, but she hated housework and had no idea about cooking.

Previous page: One of the first "glamor" publicity poses of Marilyn, for her role in *Ladies of the Chorus*.

Opposite: Even at an early age Norma Jeane Baker was not camera-shy. Her she is as a toddler, sitting on the Bolenders' Model A Ford.

Right: A chorus girl at Columbia...

Like many young husbands, Jim saw nothing wrong with seeing his friends regularly, which his wife perceived as a rejection of her company. He found it difficult to cope with her extreme sensitivity and insecurity. When he was posted to Catalina Island, where he trained new recruits, another complication came into play, as Norma Jeane attracted scores of admirers. She had no thought of being unfaithful, but Jim was still jealous.

Once Jim was posted abroad, Norma Jeane returned to live with his mother, Ethel, who found her a job at her own workplace, the Radio Plane munitions factory. It was here that army photographer David Conover spotted her, featuring her in many of the shots he took of women doing war work. He was so impressed by her ability to look good on camera that he came back to take more photographs, and suggested that she should try a career as a model. Norma Jeane needed little encouragement, and she soon signed up with the Blue Book Agency, based in Sunset Boulevard and run by Miss

Emmeline Snively. The Blue Book not only found modeling assignments, it also ran classes in makeup, grooming, posing and fashion work, the cost of which was deducted from models' fees. Norma Jeane was an apt and willing pupil - although she was still juggling these new commitments with her job at Radio Plane. Miss Snively persuaded her new signing to bleach her hair blonde, to improve her appearance in photographs and increase demand for her services.

As she became successful, Norma Jeane gave up her old job and moved out of her mother-in-law's house and into an apartment - mainly because Ethel disapproved of her new career and growing independence. Inevitably Norma Jeane's new life soon led to the end of her marriage to Jim, although they did not officially divorce until September 1946.

Meanwhile, Norma Jeane was introduced to the National Concert Artists Corporation, who became her agents and arranged her first screen test with Twentieth

Left: The publicity office came up with "interesting" stories to catch the eye of the Press, and one of the first about Marilyn was that she was a babysitter who had been "discovered". To fit this, she is pictured reading to twin babies Eric and Dick.

Below: A few years later it was older boys who were more interested in the young Marilyn...

Century Fox in July 1946. Fox offered her a standard six-month contract, with a salary of $75 per week and an option to renew for another six months at twice this. Grace McKee had to sign on Norma Jeane's behalf, as she was still under age. Ben Lyon, head of talent at the studio, also decided that she had to change her name. Norma Jeane wanted to keep the name Jean, and picked Monroe as her surname, after her grandmother. Lyon then suggested her first name should be Marilyn, after stage actress Marilyn Miller. Norma Jeane went along with this - but years later she said she never liked her new name and wished she had held out for Jean.

Although she now seemed to be on her way to stardom, Marilyn Monroe was to find that the struggle was not over yet. In her first year under contract she had only three bit parts in B-movies, despite having appeared at hundreds of Press calls and photo opportunities. Although Fox had picked up their first option, at the end of the year they declined to renew and Marilyn was out on the Hollywood circuit again, along with thousands of other aspiring starlets. Refusing to give up, she carried on modeling but also cultivated as many film contacts as possible. At one of countless Hollywood parties she was introduced to Joe Schenck, co-founder of Fox and a very influential ally, who soon persuaded Columbia Studios to hire her on a six-month contract in March 1948. At Columbia, she met drama teacher Natasha Lytess, who took her in hand and later became her personal drama coach, and was given her first proper movie role. *In Ladies of the Chorus*, she played Peggy Martin, a chorus girl desperate to marry her socialite boyfriend, and also had her first chance to sing. Despite good reviews, this time Marilyn's contract option was not picked up in September.

At this point Marilyn may have despaired, but she soon had a piece of good fortune. At a New Year's Eve Party she met influential agent Johnny Hyde, who was very taken with her and soon invited her out. He not only came to adore Marilyn, he also seemed able to see a star quality in her that others had failed to spot. From this point on, Marilyn's career took a turn for the better. Shortly afterwards she had a small, but significant part in the Marx Brothers', *Love Happy*, followed by a role as a chorus girl in *A Ticket to Tomahawk*. By August, Johnny was her agent and had turned his full attention to nurturing her career. A small part in her first high-profile picture, *The Asphalt Jungle* directed by John Huston,

began to get her noticed and not long after that she landed a good role in *All About Eve*. This movie was one of the most successful of 1950, and it brought Marilyn to the attention of Fox studio head Darryl Zanuck, and Johnny Hyde was finally able to get her that elusive long-term contract.

Throughout this period, Johnny Hyde had been urging her to marry him - he had left his wife soon after meeting Marilyn and had introduced her to top Hollywood society, as well as paying for minor cosmetic surgery and a wardrobe of good clothes. Not only was he in love with her, he was suffering from heart disease and was worried about what would happen to her after he was gone. If she had married him Marilyn would have been a rich woman, but she consistently refused. Partly because she didn't want to marry someone she didn't love, partly because she was still devastated that her voice coach, Fred Karger, had refused to marry her, and finally because she feared she would never be taken seriously as an actress if she was Mrs Johnny Hyde. The decision was to cost her dear - that December, Johnny died suddenly of a massive heart attack. Marilyn was heartbroken - although she had not loved Johnny, she had cared very deeply for him. His family immediately repossessed everything he had bought her and they threw her out of his home, then after the funeral his associates at the agency refused to take her calls. Marilyn was left in limbo - she had her contract, but it was coming up for renewal and she had no one to protect her interests.

Once again, she refused to give up, and took matters back into her own hands. After catching the attention of Spyros Skouras, president of Fox, by attending an exhibitors' dinner in a skin-tight cocktail dress, her contract was renewed. During 1951, Marilyn appeared in several rather insignificant movies for Fox, but in August the studio agreed to loan her to RKO, to film *Clash by Night*, directed by Fritz Lang. This was the first proper dramatic part that she had ever been given, with a top director, and although her role was just a supporting part she made the most of it, getting some excellent reviews. It was her performance in this movie that finally made Fox sit up and take notice, and decide that perhaps she was ready for a leading role.

Opposite: A demure-looking Marilyn poses in a sexy, strapless gown. At this point in her career she was still one of hundreds of aspiring starlets.

Norma Jeane

Opposite: An early picture of Marilyn at the beach, when she was still a teenager called Norma Jeane Baker. Despite her youth, she already instinctively knew how to pose for the camera.

Above: The young Norma Jeane was persuaded to join the Blue Book Agency, after photographer David Conover discovered her doing war work in the Radio Plane munitions factory. She was in demand as a model, and it was not long before she was also taken on by National Concert Artists Corporation. A screen test at Fox followed, and a standard six-month contract. It was Ben Lyon at Fox who changed the budding starlet's name to Marilyn Monroe.

A Star is Born...

Right: James Dougherty, Marilyn's first husband. They had married in June 1942, just three weeks after her 16th birthday, but the relationship was short-lived. Marilyn later told reporters that her first marriage had been a mistake, but Jim believed they would have remained together had he not been sent away on active service less than two years after their wedding. Their divorce was made final in September 1946.

Opposite: To create interest in their new starlet, the Fox publicity department concocted a story that Marilyn had been discovered when she had been hired as a babysitter for a casting director and Marilyn was pictured reading a story to three-year-old Joanne Metzler. Stories like these made hundreds of young girls believe that they too could be discovered, if only they were in the right place at the right time.

Below: A publicity photograph released at the same time as Marilyn's first movie - a bit part in *Scudda Hoo, Scudda Hay*, which was filmed during the course of her first year under contract at Twentieth Century Fox. Marilyn's part was mostly cut before the movie was released in April 1948, so she only appears in the distance in one shot.

Smile, please...

Left: The publicity department took an endless series of "cheesecake" photos of all the Fox contract players. Marilyn was always ready to appear for a photographic session, as she knew her future career depended on being noticed by somebody in a position of power. She was successful in this, first becoming one of Joseph M. Schenck's "girls" and then catching the eye of influential agent Johnny Hyde.

Right: Sometimes the publicity pictures took on a more practical aspect, as in this "how to look like a movie-star" beauty session, in which Marilyn is shown applying makeup for the cameras.

Below: Another part of the budding starlet's life was a succession of classes, in which they learned acting, singing and dancing, as well as studying movement and voice culture. In contrast to her screen image, in reality Marilyn was no dizzy blonde and worked hard to improve her acting technique, studying at the Actors' Lab off Sunset Boulevard and seeking to perfect every aspect of her performance.

Ladies of the Chorus

Right: In 1948 Marilyn was briefly under contract to Columbia Studios, and had a part in *Ladies of the Chorus*. She played singer Peggy Martin (third from the right, front row) and Adele Jergens (center, back row) played her mother, although she was only just over eight years older than Marilyn. This was Marilyn's first co-starring role, but it was only a low-budget "B" movie so it made little impact on her career.

However, the picture was significant in that Columbia Studios' drama coach, Natasha Lytess, was assigned to work with Marilyn on her portrayal of the burlesque singer. Natasha was soon to become Marilyn's personal teacher and her advice and support quickly became indispensable to her insecure pupil.

Love conquers all?

Left : A still from *Ladies of the Chorus*, in which Marilyn receives a corsage from an admirer. The movie gave her a chance to sing for the first time, and she was assigned to voice coach Fred Karger. She fell in love with Karger, but he refused to marry her, later marrying actress Jane Wyman instead.

Right: Marilyn gazes lovingly into the eyes of Rand Brooks, who played her handsome socialite boyfriend, Randy Carroll, in the movie. The plot has the two of them planning to marry, despite the social divide which threatens to keep them apart. In the end love conquers all.

Below: Posing for illustrator Earl Moran. Moran was one of America's most renowned cheesecake artists and Marilyn modeled for him regularly between 1946 and 1949, earning $10 an hour. It was steady work that kept her going as she tried to break into the movie business. Moran produced several charcoal and chalk pictures of her that featured on various calendars.

Johnny's girl

Opposite: Ladies of the Chorus was shot in only ten days. Marilyn told reporters later that when the movie was released, she was so excited that she drove past the theater several times to see her name on the marquee. She wished that it said "Norma Jeane" rather than "Marilyn Monroe", so that all the people who had ignored her in the past could see it.

Above: Unfortunately Columbia Studios chief Harry Cohn was not so impressed with her performance, and Marilyn's option was not picked up. However, Marilyn had been taken under the wing of William Morris agent Johnny Hyde, a well-connected Hollywood player who had managed Rita Hayworth. Johnny introduced Marilyn into his social circle and contributed financially to ensure that his protégée looked the part, paying for some minor cosmetic surgery and for hairdressers to color her hair.

A ticket to ride...

A Ticket to Tomahawk was
Marilyn's first movie for
Twentieth Century Fox since
they had declined to pick up
her option two years earlier.
The movie was a rather low-
key musical Western and did
little for her career - but it
would have done much better
if it had been properly
promoted. Unfortunately, Fox
had just released a Betty
Grable comic Western, *The
Beautiful Blonde from Bashful
Bend*, which had been badly
reviewed and had done rather
poorly, so at the time they
were not inclined to spend
further money on publicity
for another Western that
could also prove to be a flop.

The Asphalt Jungle

Below: Johnny Hyde was instrumental in getting Marilyn the part of Angela, the mistress of a bent lawyer, in *The Asphalt Jungle.* John Huston's movie was a commerical success but unusual in two ways: it portrayed criminals as ordinary people rather than as gangsters and, more importantly, he had decided not to include any established stars in the cast. Marilyn only had three scenes but she certainly made an impact. Here she is pictured with Sam Jaffe, who played Doc Riedenschneider, the criminal who sets up the jewel heist that the plot hinges on.

Opposite: Louis Calhern played the lawyer, Alonzo D. Emmerich. In the movie, Angela gives him a false alibi for the jewel heist, but when she is questioned by the police her loyalty wavers. Her big dramatic scene was shot in only two takes.

Right: Marilyn with her co-star Dan Dailey in *A Ticket to Tomahawk.* She played one of four chorus girls in a story that involved a stage-coach owner trying to stop the new-fangled railroad from ruining his business.

All About Eve...

Johnny Hyde was also instrumental in getting Marilyn cast in *All About Eve*, starring Bette Davis and directed by Joseph L. Mankiewicz. Hyde taught Marilyn that it was better to have a small part in a good movie with an excellent director, than a leading role in a poor movie with a mediocre one. It was this lesson that led to her battle to obtain director and script approval in later years.

Opposite: A publicity shot for Fox's newest star - but despite her growing box-office appeal she was still on a basic salary.

Right: With Thanksgiving approaching in November 1950, the Press office saw an ideal opportunity to talk turkey...

Below: Anne Baxter, Bette Davis, Marilyn and George Sanders in a scene from *All About Eve*. Marilyn played aspiring actress Claudia Caswell, and was introduced by Sanders as "a graduate of the Copacabana school of acting". Although her part was small, it was crucial to highlight the contrasting characters of Eve, played by Anne Baxter, and Margo, played by Bette Davis. The picture went on to receive 14 Academy Award nominations and won Best Movie, while Mankiewicz took Best Director and George Saunders was awarded Best Supporting Actor.

Pin-up

The editors of *Stars and Stripes*, the newspaper for U.S. occupation forces, voted unanimously to award the title of Miss Cheesecake of 1950 to Marilyn. The 1st Marine Division also christened her Miss Morale as they left for Korea. She always felt that her rise to stardom was accelerated by the devotion of soldiers, for whom she was a favorite pin-up.

With a powerful patron behind her and two critically successful movies completed, it seemed that Marilyn was on the way to achieving her ambition. But at the end of 1951 Johnny Hyde died of a heart attack and Marilyn found herself alone and dependent on her own resources again.

Miss Valentine

Opposite: Publicity poses were usually glamor shots, as Fox began to see Marilyn as a replacement for Betty Grable, who was nearing the end of her career. However, Marilyn was still roped in to do her share of opportunistic poses...

Right: For Valentine's Day 1951, she was dressed in a sexy two-piece cowgirl costume and posed with a heart-shaped target.

Below: Although Marilyn only had a small part in *As Young As You Feel*, her name was billed above the title to capitalize on her recent success. It had also convinced studio head Darryl Zanuck to finally offer her a long-term contract. In a scene from the movie, Marilyn, as Harriet, takes dictation from industry boss Louis McKinley, played by Albert Dekker. It was on the set of *As Young As You Feel*, while she was still grieving over the death of Johnny Hyde, that Elia Kazan introduced Marilyn to the playwright Arthur Miller - an encounter that Marilyn did not forget.

Muscle toning...

Marilyn goes through her exercise routine for the benefit of photographers. She told them that you needed to put a lot of effort into the routine, to really exercise most of the muscles in the body, and that she admired the way French women walked. "They don't just plod down streets like so many horses - they jiggle, they bounce, they weave - they come to life."

In her early career she was concerned about a healthy lifestyle and keeping fit and often went running in the morning. In later years this habit slipped as the sleeplessness, drugs and insecurity began to take their toll.

Marilyn was working on *Home Town Story* when she heard that she had secured a seven-year contract with Twentieth Century Fox. Although this gave her the security of a weekly salary regardless of whether or not she worked, it also meant that the studio had control over her career. She would not be permitted to work on stage, radio or television unless sanctioned by Fox and she could be lent out to another studio if such an arrangement suited studio boss Darryl Zanuck. During the first year her salary was set at $500 a month and was due to rise steadily to $3,500 by the time the contract expired.

Above: When she was voted "the present all GIs would like to find in their Christmas stocking", the Fox Press office swung into action to photograph Marilyn amply filling an oversize stocking.

Opposite: The title of Cheesecake Queen provided the opportunity to feature her plunging a sword into a cheesecake, at a party given by Michael Gaszynski, a former Polish diplomat who was celebrating the passing of his American citizenship exams.

CHAPTER TWO

Gentlemen Prefer Blondes

Although at the end of 1951 Fox did try Marilyn as the lead in a serious drama - *Don't Bother to Knock* - it was not very successful commercially and she was soon back in light comedy roles. The first of these was *Monkey Business*, a screwball comedy in which Marilyn played the only sane character. When it was released, it was a measure of her growing popularity that theater owners often featured her name to publicize the movie, rather than those of her more famous co-stars, Cary Grant and Ginger Rogers.

Whenever Marilyn worked, her personal drama coach, Natasha Lytess, had to be near by on the set. Marilyn originally met Natasha at Columbia, where she had been the drama coach assigned to help the young starlet prepare for her role in *Ladies of the Chorus*. When Marilyn had signed her new contract with Fox, the only privilege she had asked for was that Natasha should be hired as her personal drama coach, and to work with other contract players when possible. Marilyn's reliance on Natasha often drove her directors and co-stars mad. Rather than looking to the director at the end of a take, she sought Natasha's approval - and if she didn't get it she would ask for a retake. Directors resented a second authority usurping their own, while other actors were put under pressure, as they knew that the take used would be the best one of Marilyn, so they had to be good every time.

While Marilyn was working on *Monkey Business*, a potential disaster loomed. In May 1949, she had posed nude for photographer Tom Kelley, and the picture had been used anonymously on a 1952 calendar - which now adorned gas stations and barbershops across the country. Someone had recognized Marilyn as the blonde stretched out artistically on red velvet, and the story was about to break in the Press. In the moral climate of the early 1950s, the scandal could have ruined her budding career - posing nude was not something a nice girl did, and no Hollywood star had ever been caught out behaving in such a way. Fox executives were all for denying the whole thing, but Marilyn thought she should just tell the truth and admit everything - and for the first time, her view prevailed. An exclusive interview was arranged with journalist Aline Mosby, and the story ran in U.S. newspapers in March. Marilyn confessed that she was the blonde, and explained that she had desperately needed the money to pay off debts and that this had been the only honest way she could earn it quickly. She mentioned that the photographer's wife had been present at the shoot, and said that she felt she had done nothing to be ashamed of. The result was a triumph, instead of a disaster. Public sympathy swung behind her and the calendar was reprinted many times during the early fifties - it is estimated that as many as four million copies were sold.

Two days after the story broke, Marilyn met baseball star Joe DiMaggio for the first time. He had seen a publicity photo of her with two White Sox players, and asked who she was. Later he discovered that one of his drinking buddies knew her and could arrange an introduction. After dinner he called her every night and they were soon a famous couple, with their romance documented in all the newspapers. Marilyn loved the warmth of his Italian family and valued the feeling of security he gave her, and the impression that he was batting on her side.

She certainly needed support, as within a couple of months another potential threat to her career appeared. All the publicity about Marilyn as she became a star had been built around the fact that she was an orphan, who had become successful despite adversity. Now a journalist had tracked down her mother - who was not only still alive, but had just been released from the latest in a series of state mental institutions. Coming just after the "nude calendar" revelations, the timing could not have been worse. Marilyn quickly gave another exclusive interview, this time to Erskine Johnson, saying that she had not known as a child, when she had spent time in an orphanage and in foster homes, that her mother was in hospital. She also said that, having discovered that her mother was still alive, she had been in contact and was offering help as required. The last part at least was true - Marilyn's business manager, Inez Melson, had been visiting Gladys to make sure she had sufficient money since 1951. Again, the explanation was accepted and Marilyn retained her public following.

Meanwhile, she was about to begin work on her next major starring role. In *Niagara*, she played a sultry seductress who plans to murder her husband so she can be with her lover. The scene where Marilyn croons along with a record was so sexually charged that it outraged representatives from the Women's Clubs of America, and had to be hastily modified. Throughout filming, Marilyn pushed the limits of what was acceptable, and she outshone the more experienced actors with whom she was working. When she was on the screen, the audience didn't look at anyone else. After the picture was completed, everyone was left in no doubt that Marilyn was truly a star.

In 1952, five movies featuring Marilyn were released - *Clash by Night* for RKO and *We're Not Married*, *Don't Bother to Knock*, *Monkey Business* and *O Henry's Full House* for Fox. Her next picture for Fox was already lined up. The studio had originally bought the rights to *Gentlemen Prefer Blondes* for Betty Grable, but director Howard Hawks, who had recently worked with Marilyn on *Monkey Business*, was convinced she was perfect for the part of Lorelei Lee. Despite some studio reservations as to whether she was up to the demands of the role, she was paired with Jane Russell and at the beginning of November 1952 work started on costume and makeup tests. In this movie, Marilyn has a far more polished and sophisticated look than she had achieved before - and this is often attributed to the influence of Hawks. For the dance numbers, Marilyn worked hard with choreographer Jack Cole to perfect her technique, because she knew she had no natural ability here, as she did with acting and singing.

By now, Marilyn was beginning to cause problems on set with her chronic lateness. She would arrive at the studio early, but was still locked in her dressing room hours after filming was due to start. It was a habit that often drove her directors and co-workers crazy, because they saw it as evidence of unprofessionalism, laziness or as deliberate rudeness. However, on this movie co-star Jane Russell soon realized the cause. It wasn't that Marilyn would not come to the set - she couldn't. She was terrified of going in front of the camera, because she could not bear the thought of failing, of being less than perfect. She spent hours doing and re-doing her makeup, and working herself up to the point at which she could perform. It was this very intensity with which she approached her roles that came over on the screen, and made her such a unique star. Jane provided a simple and fairly effective solution - every morning she would stop by Marilyn's dressing room and collect her. Once on set, Marilyn would work, as long as the atmosphere was conducive, and as long as Natasha was on hand.

The following year, 1953, was one of the high points in Marilyn's career. In January, *Niagara* was released and went on to earn more than five times what it had cost to make, confirming Marilyn as a top box-office draw. In April she began work on another major role, co-starring in *How to Marry a Millionaire*. In this, she was working with two well-established stars, Betty Grable and Lauren Bacall. The studio made much of a supposed feud between

Previous page: Marilyn and Jane Russell strike a pose in *Gentlemen Prefer Blondes*.

Opposite: Although she was the blonde, Marilyn was being paid far less than Jane Russell was, as she was still locked into her studio contract on a weekly salary.

Marilyn and Betty - the incoming star and the outgoing one - but in fact they got on well and became great friends. Although she had been dubious about playing the part of a girl who wore glasses, the "accidents" built round her character's short-sightedness confirmed Marilyn's talent as an actress with a gift for comedy.

In July, *Gentlemen Prefer Blondes* was released, and it quickly became a spectacular success. Both the public and the critics loved it and it brought Marilyn her first awards for her talent, rather than her looks - *Photoplay* magazine's Best Actress of 1953, and Best Friend a Diamond Ever Had award from the Jewelry Academy.

As part of the publicity campaign, Marilyn and Jane Russell were invited to leave their prints outside Grauman's Chinese Theater on Hollywood Boulevard. The tradition had begun when Mary Pickford and Douglas Fairbanks had accidentally stepped into some wet concrete outside the theater, and Grauman had suggested they add their signatures to the footprints. Marilyn went to the theater when she was a child, and had tried to fit her feet into the stars' prints as she daydreamed about becoming famous herself. So the occasion really was a dream come true. She had asked for a diamond to dot the "i" in her name, but settled for a rhinestone - which very soon caught the eye of a souvenir hunter and was stolen.

Marilyn had gone straight from *Gentlemen Prefer Blondes* to *How to Marry a Millionaire*, with little rest in between, and now she was about to start on *River of No Return*. Charles Feldman of Famous Artists, who was acting as her agent although she had not signed the contract, was becoming concerned about the effect of continuous working on her health

Left: To publicize the July release of *Gentlemen Prefer Blondes*, Marilyn appeared in a campaign to promote safety during 4th July celebrations.

Opposite: Marilyn shows off some of her assets.

- and was worried that her career might be damaged by overexposure. When the studio informed her that immediately after *River of No Return* they intended to put her in another musical, *The Girl in Pink Tights*, Feldman advised her to turn the project down. He also thought that this would signal to studio executives that he and Marilyn were aware of just how important she had become, as a prelude to renegotiating her contract. On one hand Marilyn was reluctant to turn down an assignment because of her insecurity, and because she had no savings to tide her over if the studio suspended her, but on the other she had her own worries about accepting the movie. Firstly, she was annoyed that no one thought it important that she should see the script - she had only been sent a précis of the plot - and from that, it was evident that the character was similar to those she had played in her last two pictures. This fueled another worry - she was afraid of being typecast and outliving her usefulness, so she wanted to play a wider range of roles. In addition to the studio choosing all her projects with no reference to her, they were also assigning the director, and Marilyn had learned how important it was to work with directors who could bring out the best in her. Lastly, yet again she was being expected to star in a movie for her usual salary of $1,500 a week - negotiated way back in 1951 before she had become a star - while her co-star, Frank Sinatra, would be paid $5,000 a week. She went off to Canada for location filming on *River of No Return* with these issues still unresolved.

Marilyn had another problem to sort out. Joe DiMaggio had several times asked her to marry him, but she couldn't make up her mind what to do. She loved him and valued the stability and support he offered - but he was not interested in art and books, as she was, and was incredibly jealous of any attention she received from other men. Most of their arguments were to do with her need for public adulation and her habit of dressing provocatively. More importantly, he wanted her to give up the movies and become a beautiful, ex-movie-star housewife, while she was still focused on obtaining the respect and adulation in her career that she felt she deserved. They decided that Joe should join her in Canada, and away from the stresses of Hollywood they would try to come to a decision.

The filming of *River of No Return* was not a happy experience for many of those concerned. Director Otto Preminger made little secret of his lack of enthusiasm for the project and took a great dislike to Natasha Lytess. When Natasha upset child actor Tommy Rettig, causing him to forget his lines, Preminger banned her from the set, although Marilyn quietly made sure that the studio reinstated her. Both Marilyn and co-star Robert Mitchum had physically demanding roles, and part of the plot involved traveling down rapids on a raft, which meant that they had to spend a great deal of time doused in water for continuity.

Marilyn, who usually got on well with children, was surprised that Tommy Rettig avoided her off set. She asked him why, and was devastated to discover that he had been told by his priest that it was fine to work with "a woman like her", but implied that he should not socialize with her. Luckily things improved between them after DiMaggio arrived, as Tommy was impressed that such a famous baseball star obviously respected Marilyn and the three of them even went fishing together.

After filming finished, Joe took Marilyn off to spend a few days with his family in San Francisco, and then they returned to Hollywood. Although he wanted her to give up the movies, he could understand her battles with the studio - particularly over money. Money meant respect - so the more money they were prepared to pay, the more they respected you. On the matter of *The Girl in Pink Tights*, Marilyn was now ready to give in and start work on the movie. Natasha had been pressurizing her to accept it, because she was afraid that if Marilyn didn't, her own position on the Fox payroll would be put in jeopardy, while Feldman didn't think it was that important if Marilyn felt she had to do it. However, at this point DiMaggio proved what an astute businessman he was, by pointing out that if Marilyn refused the movie, Fox would have no backlog of Monroe pictures to release, thus putting Feldman in a much stronger bargaining position. When the first day of shooting arrived, Marilyn failed to appear on set.

Opposite: Marilyn first appeared on *The Jack Benny Show* in September 1953, and afterwards she and Benny became great friends. Marilyn did the show to publicize her films, but since her contract with Fox did not allow her to receive cash for this type of work she was given a black Cadillac convertible with a red interior instead.

Clash by Night

Above: Marilyn poses with actor Keith Andes, who played her love-interest in *Clash by Night*, which was released in 1952. She had been loaned out by Fox to RKO and it was her first major role in which some serious acting was required. Along with Barbara Stanwyck, Marilyn would have her name above the titles. She insisted that her personal drama coach, Natasha Lytess, was present on set, which did not please director Fritz Lang, although eventually a compromise was reached. Determined to impress, she employed acting teacher Michael Chekhov in addition to working on the part with Natasha.

We're Not Married

Actor David Wayne looks stony-faced as Marilyn gives him a peck on the cheek in a scene from *We're Not Married* which had a star-studded cast including Ginger Rogers, Fred Allen and Zsa Zsa Gabor. The movie told the stories of five different couples who find out some time after the wedding that they are not legally married because the judge's license was not valid. Marilyn plays a housewife who enters the Mrs America beauty pageant. Her role was hastily added to the storyline to cash in on her growing popularity, and scriptwriter Nunnally Johnson later admitted he had deliberately created opportunities for her to appear in two bathing costumes.

Right: One of the bathing costumes from *We're Not Married* was reused for a Fox publicity still, when Marilyn posed for yet another Valentine picture for the U.S. armed forces.

Opposite: Swimsuit glamor girl... : Although the studio had begun to cast her in a steady stream of pictures, Marilyn had not forgotten the importance of publicity and was still prepared to pose for photographers. It would not be long though before she yearned to escape from the "blonde bombshell" image.

Dating Joe DiMaggio

Above: Joe DiMaggio talks to newsmen in the Press room at Yankee Stadium just before a game is due to start. He and Marilyn met on a date in March 1952 at the Villa Nova restaurant, and soon became an item in the Press.

Left: DiMaggio had taken his ten-year-old son, Joe Jr., to meet Marilyn, and they had got on well - Marilyn had an empathy with most children. However, Joe's ex-wife, actress Dorothy Arnold, was furious and told newspapermen that she intended asking the courts to modify her divorce to stop such visits, because Joe Jr. had come home talking of Marilyn's "beautiful legs" and calling her a "doll".

Opposite: Marilyn checks out her appearance. Later she would spend hours in front of the mirror before appearing on set - not because she was vain, but because she couldn't bring herself to appear until she thought everything was absolutely perfect.

A screwball comedy

Opposite: Marilyn appears in a swimsuit and (above) with Cary Grant in publicity stills for *Monkey Business* filmed at the start of 1952. The movie was a screwball comedy starring Cary Grant and Ginger Rogers but shortly before shooting began studio boss Darryl Zanuck asked the scriptwriters to expand both Marilyn's part and that of the monkey!

Marilyn played a dumb blonde secretary, and Grant a scientist who is trying to invent an elixir of youth. One of the laboratory monkeys mixes a formula and puts it in the water cooler - and of course this turns out to be the youth potion that everyone is seeking. Several characters then unknowingly drink the potion and revert to their childhood, providing the writers with plenty of opportunity for comedy.

A visit from Joe

When Joe DiMaggio visited the set he was photographed with Cary Grant and Marilyn - but newspaper editors cropped out Cary Grant and photographs of Joe and Marilyn were sent around the world. Costume designer William Travilla, who worked with Marilyn on many movies, said that of all the outfits that he had created for her this beige jersey dress which she wears in her opening scenes in *Monkey Business* was her least favorite.

A little Monkey Business...

The swimsuit poses were at least related to the plot of the picture - after Barnaby Fulton (Cary Grant) drinks the youth potion he rushes out and buys a sports car, and then takes Lois Laurel (Marilyn) for a spin and they end up going swimming.

While she was filming *Monkey Business*, Marilyn developed appendicitis but she refused to go into hospital for an operation until the end of April after she had completed her part. However, although she was prepared to put up with a lot of pain in order to retain her part in the movie, she was reputedly regularly late arriving on set, a habit that was to become more pronounced in the years to come. Howard Hawks later said of her that she was "late every day...but she knew all her lines".

Opposite: Marilyn signs an autograph for a fan. Later a group of New York-based fans were known as the Monroe Six, and they were always present when she was due to appear. When she lived in New York they followed her around, tipping each other off as to what she was doing. She valued their devotion, and once invited all of them to a picnic at Roxbury, where she was living with Arthur Miller.

Calm before a storm

Marilyn relaxes in the sun on the terrace of her home in Hollywood. However, just as she had finally realized her childhood ambitions, playing opposite Cary Grant in a Howard Hawks movie, her past came back to haunt her. Marilyn had been recognized as the nude model in a calendar which had been distributed all over the U.S. and the morality clause in her contract allowed the studio to dismiss her should the public react unfavorably to this revelation. Poised on the verge of success, Marilyn was in danger of losing everything she had striven so hard to achieve. However, in contrast to the advice of the studio publicists, Marilyn's instinct was to admit that she had modeled for the pictures, pleading poverty as the motive. The public forgave her and the publicity only increased her profile.

As early as 1952, Marilyn was already being thought of by many as just a dumb blonde. It was a stereotype that infuriated her, as it prevented her being considered for more serious acting roles. Part of this was due to studio head Darryl Zanuck, who considered Marilyn to be "empty-headed", but it is debatable whether Marilyn would have risen so high so fast if her early screen roles had been more varied. As it was, she quickly developed a persona that the public loved - and then spent the rest of her career trying to get away from it.

Miss America...

Since *Monkey Business* opened in Atlantic City, home of the Miss America beauty pageant, Marilyn was invited to be Grand Marshal - the first woman to appear in the honorary role. She took part wearing a low-cut dress that was very revealing, and when the inevitable storm burst a few days later she coyly commented, "People were staring down at me all day long, but I thought they were admiring my Grand Marshal badge." Joe deeply disapproved of Marilyn's selection of such immodest attire and was angered when pictures appeared in the Press.

Niagara Falls

In her second leading role, Marilyn shared star billing only with Niagara Falls. She played Rose Loomis, who plans to murder her husband, played by Joseph Cotten, so she can be with her lover. The plan goes wrong, and both Rose and her lover end up dead. The movie featured what was the longest walk in screen history at the time - 116 feet of Marilyn swiveling her hips provocatively as she moved away from the camera, wearing a tight black skirt. It caused a sensation - but Marilyn told readers of *Life* magazine, "I've been walking since I was six months old - I just use it to get me around."

Left: Marilyn proves she really could look good in any old thing...

Opposite: Marilyn with Henry Hathaway, director of *Niagara*. Although he was notorious for shouting at actors, he was concerned about Marilyn, not only looking after her on set but advising her to get a good agent to limit the endless publicity demands on her time.

Gentlemen Prefer Blondes

Above: Marilyn arrives in New York in October 1952 to publicize *Monkey Business*. However, this would be one of the few public appearances she would make for some months. After years of tirelessly seeking publicity to advance her career, the studio signaled a new confidence in her and Marilyn was instructed to concentrate solely on preparing for her new role in Howard Hawks' latest project, *Gentlemen Prefer Blondes,* based on the book by Anita Loos.

Having already directed Marilyn in *Monkey Business*, Howard Hawks understood that comedy, rather than drama was her forte. He persuaded Darryl Zanuck, head of production at Fox, that the combination of established Jane Russell and popular newcomer Marilyn Monroe could be successful at the box office. On her 26th birthday Marilyn was thrilled to be offered the part of Lorelei, created on Broadway by Carol Channing.

Above: Marilyn's drama coach Natasha Lytess explains a point between takes.

Right: Jane Russell with Marilyn on the set of *Gentlemen Prefer Blondes*. The two stars got on very well together - even though Russell was being paid ten times what Marilyn earned for making the movie under her standard studio contract.

Two little girls from Little Rock...

Jane and Marilyn play two showgirls traveling to France on a cruise liner, where Lorelei is to marry her wealthy boyfriend, Gus Esmond. Esmond Sr. is convinced Lorelei is a gold digger, and hires a private detective to prove it. Marilyn was determined not to squander the opportunity offered to her. She worked late into the evenings to perfect Jack Cole's dance routines. Together the girls performed the show's opening number "Two Little Girls from Little Rock" but the best-remembered song in the movie is Marilyn's rendition of "Diamonds Are a Girl's Best Friend".

Above: After seeing a diamond tiara belonging to Lady Beekman, Lorelei tries out a napkin ring for effect, commenting that she loves to find new places to wear diamonds.

Left: Newcomer Tommy Noonan played the wealthy playboy, Gus Esmond. His rather naive character stood little chance against the wiles of blonde bombshell Lorelei.

Diamonds are a girl's best friend

Above: Irene Crosby, Marilyn's stand-in on *Gentlemen Prefer Blondes*, poses with the star. On set Marilyn had gathered around her a small group of people with whom she had a strong rapport. Natasha was always present, but loyal makeup man Whitey Snyder and hairdresser Gladys Whitten were also there to encourage and support her.

Opposite: Diamonds are a girl's best friend... Marilyn poses with thousands of dollars' worth of real diamonds to publicize *Gentlemen Prefer Blondes*. In real life, Marilyn did not care much for expensive jewelry and owned very little. The items she wears in her Press photographs are all borrowed from the studio or from jewelers.

Worst-tressed actress

Opposite: Marilyn's looks were not admired by everyone. Hairdressers in America voted her America's "Worst Tressed" actress saying that her hair looked like a "shaggy dog". They suggested she should cut at least three inches off. Elizabeth Taylor was voted "Best Tressed" at the same time, for being "glamorously trim".

Right: Marilyn's hair color was naturally a rich red-brown and quite curly. During her career as a blonde, she went through every shade from golden to platinum.

Above: Marilyn studies some of theater-director Max Reinhardt's original manuscripts, which she had recently acquired at auction, paying $1,335. Her interest in the papers no doubt stemmed from the fact that Natasha Lytess had been part of Reinhardt's theater company in Germany. Marilyn's purchase caused the Press to complain that she had deprived a university library of the chance to have the manuscripts, which would have meant they were available for all students to study. Marilyn replied that she was thinking of donating them. However, Reinhardt's son acquired them from her at cost - and then sold them on at a handsome profit.

Dressed to impress...

Leading Hollywood costume designer William Travilla - known simply as Travilla - designed many of the dresses that Marilyn wore in her movies, including the outfits for *Gentlemen Prefer Blondes*. But both Howard Hawks and Travilla could take credit for the slick and sophisticated costumes in the picture which helped change Marilyn's image on screen. Travilla also designed many of the memorable dresses she wore to public events. She had very few formal clothes of her own - whenever she needed to dress up she would borrow something from the studio wardrobe.

Above: No sooner had Marilyn dealt with the crisis over the calendar photographs, when her mother came back to haunt her - the publicity office at Fox had told the Press that Marilyn was an orphan, but a persistent reporter tracked Gladys Baker down and found out she had recently been released from a state mental hospital.

Opposite top: Gossip columnist Walter Winchell, Marilyn and Joe Schenck at a party for Winchell's birthday at Ciro's in Hollywood in May 1953. Winchell was also a friend of Joe DiMaggio.

Opposite bottom: Marilyn and Jane Russell were invited to leave their prints outside Grauman's Chinese Theater as part of the publicity for the release of *Gentlemen Prefer Blondes*. Marilyn jokingly suggested that they should leave imprints of what they were famous for instead - her behind and Russell's chest.

Best rear view

Above: Although this is a publicity photograph for *Gentlemen Prefer Blondes*, Marilyn is wearing a robe that was one of her costumes from *Niagara*. The studio often recycled costumes between different stars and different movies. After four months of filming, *Gentlemen Prefer Blondes* was completed in March 1953. Fox now recognized Marilyn's potential as a box-office draw and scheduled her to commence work on a new picture with only four days' break.

Opposite: According to movie cameraman Frank Powolny, Marilyn had the best rear view of all the stars he had photographed during his career.

How to Marry a Millionaire

Opposite and previous pages: Marilyn as Pola Debevoise in *How to Marry a Millionaire*, with co-stars Betty Grable and Lauren Bacall. The movie was designed to capitalize on the success of *Gentlemen Prefer Blondes*, although neither the script nor the direction was as accomplished as that of the Hawks musical. Marilyn was exhausted by having expended so much energy in mastering the routines on her previous picture and was further handicapped by her usual nerves in front of the camera.

Marilyn's character was terribly short-sighted but refused to wear her glasses in public, which led to a lot of comic mishaps.

Right: Jack Benny and Marilyn out on the town. After they became friends they often became involved in pranks together. At one point they reportedly visited a nudist beach, with Benny wearing a false beard and Marilyn a black wig.

Below: Spyros Skouras, president of Twentieth Century Fox, and Darryl Zanuck, co-founder and studio head. Skouras frequently championed Marilyn, while she felt Zanuck was responsible for the long string of "dumb blonde" roles she was forced to play.

On the Jack Benny Show

Opposite: Marilyn gets a hug from comedian Jack Benny in a publicity picture for her guest appearance on his show, transmitted live from the Shrine Auditorium in Los Angeles on 13 September 1953. Marilyn performed a comedy skit with Benny and sang "Bye Bye Baby" before taking the opportunity to mention the release of *How to Marry a Millionaire*. She was thought to have aquitted herself well playing opposite the very experienced Jack Benny and despite the fact that she frequently needed multiple takes when acting in movies, she did not seem unduly worried that the program was live.

Above: Marilyn being interviewed in Hollywood by United Press reporter Vern Scott.

Marilyn and Joe

Joe and Marilyn continued to date although he preferred to stay out of the limelight. He seldom accompanied her on public appearances, sometimes waiting outside to collect her at the end of the evening. The Press still speculated as to whether, and when, they would marry, but although Marilyn valued Joe's steady devotion and his close-knit family she was not ready to give up her career and all that she had struggled to achieve to be the sort of wife he wanted.

Despite starring in two of the most commercially successful films of 1953, Marilyn was living in a small rented apartment on Doheny Drive near Sunset Strip. Joe would have preferred that Marilyn did not work, but he took considerable interest in the financial and contractual discussions which followed her recent successes. Marilyn had made the leap from starlet to star and she and her advisers decided that it was time to renegotiate her contract with the studio.

Opposite: During the filming of *River of No Return* in Alberta, Canada in August 1953, Marilyn slipped on some wet rocks and damaged her leg. It had to be bandaged and she was forced to hobble around for several days. This was not the only difficulty on set. During the filming of *How to Marry a Millionaire*, director Jean Negulesco had sought to accommodate Marilyn's wishes by tolerating Natasha Lytess's interference. However, on *River of No Return*, Otto Preminger banned Natasha from the set, insisting that she remain in Marilyn's dressing room. The movie over-ran and Marilyn's co-star Robert Mitchum is said to have dubbed it "the picture of no return".

In the movie Marilyn plays Kay, a saloon singer, who ends up traveling down a river on a raft with farmer Matt Calder (Robert Mitchum) and his young son (Tommy Rettig). By a strange coincidence, Mitchum had been in the army with Marilyn's first husband, Jim Dougherty.

Below: Yet another swimsuit pose...
All the photographers that Marilyn worked with commented on how professional and dedicated she was.

Left: Trying on different outfits before posing for a photograph to promote safety during the forthcoming Independence Day celebrations.

River of No Return

Joe DiMaggio joined Marilyn in Canada while she was filming *River of No Return*. They had been dating for more than a year, but Marilyn could not make up her mind whether to marry him. He brought his friend, George Solotaire, and they went on fishing trips, sometimes accompanied by Marilyn and young Tommy Rettig.

Opposite above: Jack Benny and Marilyn, in a publicity picture for her TV debut on his show.

Opposite below: Tommy Rettig and Marilyn at a movie. After a shaky start the two of them got on well together.

CHAPTER THREE

There's No Business Like Show Business

Fox's response to Marilyn's failure to start on *The Girl in Pink Tights* was immediate. They couldn't get hold of Marilyn herself, who was lying low protected by Joe, but they contacted both her agents and Natasha. Famous Artists informed the studio that she was not ready to start on the movie because she still hadn't seen the script. Marilyn had trusted Natasha to be on her side, come what may, but in this instance - perhaps worried about losing her lucrative job - Natasha criticized Marilyn's behavior and tried to get her to relent. Marilyn never forgave her for it and although they worked together on two more pictures, from then on Natasha's days were numbered.

Meanwhile the studio asked Marilyn to report in, to shoot retakes on *River of No Return*. Everyone understood that it was one thing to refuse to start a project, and quite another to fail to finish one, thus preventing its release and costing the studio hundreds of thousands of dollars. Marilyn's first instinct was that it was a ruse to get her onto the lot, so she fled to San Francisco with Joe. However, her agents discovered that the retakes were indeed necessary, and persuaded her to return. As soon as they were completed, Marilyn returned to San Francisco and continued to sit tight. The studio had no option but to suspend her.

But there was an unexpected twist to come. Marilyn appreciated everything Joe was doing for her - far from holding himself aloof from the movie business as he had done before, now he was fully involved in sorting out her problems with the executives at Fox. Perhaps she understood this to mean that he was reconciled to her continuing her career, and she finally agreed to be his wife. They were married in San Francisco, and only on the day did Marilyn call the studio to let them know. Despite efforts to keep the wedding quiet, the Press turned up in force and pictures appeared in all the newspapers. Fox had little option but to lift the suspension - to do otherwise would have seemed churlish - and they informed Famous Artists that Marilyn should report to work at the end of January, after the honeymoon.

For more than a week, the newlyweds enjoyed the seclusion of a remote cabin in the mountains, far from civilization. Marilyn said later that it was during this period that she and Joe really got to know one another. However, at the end of January Joe had to be in New York, so they returned to Los Angeles - to find that Fox had finally sent a copy of the script for *The Girl in Pink Tights*. After reading it, Marilyn still did not want to do the movie. Now she was in the position of questioning the studio's ability to select suitable projects and the reaction was predictable. She was put back on suspension and the studio released a Press statement pointing out that her last few movies had been outstandingly successful, which was all the evidence needed that they were the best people to decide what she should work on. In the background to this public furore, Charles Feldman of Famous Artists was quietly renegotiating Marilyn's contract. She wanted more money, and approval of the script, director and cinematographer.

Since she was back on suspension again Marilyn was a free agent, so Joe invited her to come with him to Japan as a continuation of their honeymoon. They were going to Tokyo for the opening of the baseball season, but when they arrived it was Marilyn, not Joe, who was the center of attention. At a Press conference in their hotel, all the questions were directed at her and she announced that she planned to spend a few days in Korea, entertaining U.S. soldiers. Joe did not approve, but Marilyn had always been a big favorite with the troops and felt she owed much of her early success to their support.

Back in Los Angeles, Marilyn found out that Fox had agreed to drop *The Girl in Pink Tights* and instead offered her a supporting role in *There's No Business Like Show Business*, with the promise of the lead in *The Seven Year Itch* - a successful Broadway play to be directed by Billy Wilder. She was back on salary, but only until August 1954, when a new contract would come into force, giving her an additional fee of $100,000 for *The Seven Year Itch*. However, the studio refused to budge on her last requirement. It was always unlikely that they would - at Fox, Zanuck alone decided what movies were going to be made and who was going to make them. If he gave in to Marilyn, who knows what concessions others would demand in future? Marilyn scaled down her demands, asking only for approval of her choreographer and dramatic coach, but the studio would not agree to this either. Finally, however, they conceded that Marilyn should be consulted about the choice of coach and choreographer. It seemed as if matters were settled - but in fact now Marilyn knew that she would not get the creative control she wanted, she was already working on other plans.

Marilyn's character in *There's No Business Like Show Business* was hastily tacked on at the last minute, to create an alternative project she could work on instead of *The Girl in Pink Tights*. The result was not entirely successful, but the main function of the storyline was to provide a framework for the songs of Irving Berlin and the cast included established stars like Ethel Merman and singer Johnnie Ray. Marilyn worked hard on her routines, so as not to be outclassed by her more experienced song-and-dance co-stars. Unfortunately she didn't get on with the director, Walter Lang, and was suffering from the after-effects of a bout of pneumonia, caught entertaining the troops in Korea in below-freezing temperatures. Most critics agree that it is one of her less successful movies, and Marilyn was deeply upset at its lukewarm reception. She felt she had caved in to studio assertions that they knew what was best for her, and now she was being panned for it.

Since the schedule on *There's No Business Like Show Business* had overrun, Marilyn was forced to start *The Seven Year Itch* with no break in between. When she left for location filming in New York, Joe put on a good show when seeing her off at the airport, but in fact their marriage was already in trouble. Joe's jealousy had boiled over on more than one occasion - perhaps even into physical violence, according to some reports - and Marilyn was beginning to feel that she had made a big mistake. However, Joe did still love her and a few days later he followed her to New York. Generally he kept out of the way when she was working, but unfortunately he was on hand for the shooting of the famous skirt scene in *The Seven Year Itch*. As Marilyn stood over the subway grating, with her skirt blowing up almost to her waist and thousands of New Yorkers cheering and yelling, he was seen leaving the street with a grim expression on his face. When Marilyn came back to the hotel they had a furious row, and by the next morning their marriage was all but over.

Although her private life now lay in tatters, at least her professional life was coming together. In 1953, photographer Milton Greene had taken a series of pictures of her that she loved, and which seemed to capture a different Marilyn, bringing out aspects of her personality that no one else seemed to see. Since then Greene had listened to her complaints about the studio and, keen to break into movie production himself, he had suggested they form their own production company. As soon as it became obvious that Marilyn was not to get the creative control she wanted from Fox, she started talking seriously to Milton Greene about forming Marilyn Monroe Productions. With her own company she would be able to choose the roles she played and would have the control over her career that she so desperately wanted. At the same time, she planned to dispense with Famous Artists as her agents and move over to MCA, as she felt Feldman had failed to achieve even the most basic improvements to her contract.

In December 1954, Marilyn moved to New York, first staying in a hotel and then moving in with Greene and his wife at their house in Weston, Connecticut. Early the following year, Marilyn and Milton Greene held a Press conference to announce the formation of Marilyn Monroe Productions. Fox was not going to give up their biggest star without a fight, and their legal representatives

Previous page: Marilyn and Joe DiMaggio seem wonderfully happy on their wedding day, but unfortunately it was not to last.

Above: Although she was technically still on her honeymoon, in February 1954 Marilyn took some time out to entertain troops in Korea. Here she bends to talk to some of the soldiers who waited in near-freezing temperatures to hear her perform.

quickly pointed out that Marilyn was under exclusive contract to them for the next four years. However, lawyers for Marilyn Monroe Productions had studied the contracts with Fox, and found a number of anomalies and broken promises - including non-payment of the $100,000 additional fee for *The Seven Year Itch* - which they ruled meant the contract was null and void.

The legal battles were to continue throughout 1955, although halfway through the year the emphasis changed. Marilyn Monroe Productions had planned to find a financial backer to enable them to develop their own projects, but as time went by it became apparent that this was not going to happen - and meanwhile Marilyn had a lifestyle to maintain. At first, Fox had *The Seven Year Itch* in the can ready to release, but after it proved astoundingly successful they had no more Monroe films to follow it up with. At the end of December 1955, Marilyn

and Fox signed a new contract, which not only gave her a much more lucrative financial deal - including a percentage of the profits - but also the creative controls she craved, with approval of script, director and cinematographer. In addition, she was permitted to undertake one independent project each year. At the time it was an unprecedented amount of power for an actor to have, and represented the first breach in the traditional studio system.

Marilyn made no movies throughout the whole of 1955 - concentrating instead on developing her acting skills by working with Lee Strasberg at his Actors Studio. Strasberg believed that she had great talent and he was a major influence on her future acting style. At first she was too insecure to go to the general sessions at the Actors Studio, so he taught her privately at his home. He also advised her to begin psychoanalysis to release the unresolved tensions from her childhood, and Marilyn rushed to follow his instructions, starting sessions with Dr Margaret Hohenberg. Lee Strasberg also went on to provide the replacement for Natasha, in the form of his wife, Paula, who took over the role of personal drama coach on Marilyn's remaining pictures.

In New York, Marilyn was able to move around incognito when she wished, by the simple expedient of wearing casual clothes, covering her hair, and wearing dark glasses. Most of the time she found this liberating, but sometimes she couldn't resist slipping back into the Marilyn persona. Several people who witnessed the transformation were fascinated by it. At one moment she would seem like an ordinary person, hardly worthy of a second glance, and then she seemed to throw some kind of inner switch and a magnetism suddenly appeared, turning heads and causing people to flock round her.

During this time, Marilyn also became a part of New York literary life in a way she had never been in Hollywood, introduced to exclusive circles by the Greenes. She appeared at parties and first

Opposite: Marilyn on the set of *The Seven Year Itch* in New York, with director Billy Wilder (left) and co-star Tom Ewell.

Above: Marilyn breaks down in tears in the passenger seat of a Cadillac driven by her attorney, Jerry Giesler, after facing the Press during the announcement of her separation from Joe DiMaggio.

nights, and also donated her services to charity on several occasions. Despite the fact that their divorce was about to be finalized, Joe DiMaggio was also still very much on the scene: he turned up regularly in New York to take Marilyn out or to offer help and support. Reporters sometimes took this as a sign of an imminent reconciliation, but Marilyn always denied that they were anything more than just friends. Joe might have wished for more, but Marilyn in fact had already quietly begun a relationship with playwright Arthur Miller.

She and Arthur Miller had first met in Hollywood back in 1950, and after he returned to New York she had written to him several times. Miller was one of the most celebrated playwrights of the day, and had won the Pulitzer Prize for his 1948 play, *Death of a Salesman*, although he had struggled to repeat its success

subsequently. Now Marilyn was living in New York and moving in literary circles, it was only a matter of time before they would meet again. Miller had been attracted to Marilyn from the first, as she was to him, but he was married, with two young children. He didn't want to divorce his wife, and she didn't want to be a home-wrecker, so nothing further had come of it. Now, however, Miller's marriage was in trouble anyway. As they spent more and more time together - both in private and in public - the Press soon got wind of their unlikely friendship. At the first night of Miller's play, *A View from the Bridge*, Marilyn met his parents for the first time. Not long afterwards, she was invited to their home, and after she left Miller told them that she was the girl he was going to marry. Nobody really took him seriously, but within less than a year he and Marilyn were married.

Opposite: In New York during her battle with Fox for recognition and an improvement in the terms of her contract, Marilyn faced the Press to reveal her "new look".

Above: With Jacques Cemas, Sammy Davis Jr., Milton Greene and Mel Tormé at The Mocambo in 1955, where they were celebrating Davis's return to show business after his accident.

Love birds...

Although it had taken some time to come to a decision, there is no doubting the genuine feelings between Marilyn and Joe as they snuggle up to each other in the judge's chambers on their wedding day in January 1954. The wedding itself was planned as a rather low-key affair; Marilyn wore a neat chocolate-brown suit with an ermine collar and Joe a dark blue suit with the same polka dot tie he had worn on his first date with Marilyn. Joe had wanted to marry in a church, but both he and Marilyn were divorced so it was not possible. During the brief, three-minute ceremony, Marilyn promised to "love, honor and cherish" her husband - but the word "obey" was left out.

At the time of her wedding Marilyn was in dispute and on suspension from Fox, but she called the studio publicists an hour before the wedding to let them know. It was long enough for them to put the word round and - despite the happy couple's desire to keep the ceremony private - hundreds of reporters descended on San Francisco town hall after having been tipped off. The Press were excluded from the actual ceremony, but afterwards Joe and Marilyn smiled for photographers and waved to the fans as they hurried to Joe's blue Cadillac. They spent their honeymoon night at the Clifton Motel in Paso Robles, before vanishing to a hideway cabin in the mountains to spend some tranquil time walking in the woods and fishing.

En route to Tokyo...

Opposite: Joe had been invited to Tokyo to open the 1954 Japanese baseball season, and since she was back on suspension after refusing to appear in *The Girl in Pink Tights*, Marilyn decided to accompany him.

Above: During a brief stopover in Honolulu, Marilyn and Joe, along with San Diego Padre manager Lefty O'Doul, were given traditional flower leis.

Left: At a Press conference in Japan, Marilyn poses happily for photographers. Joe was not happy that his wife seemed to be getting more attention than he was - particularly as the Press call had been arranged for him.

Below: Although this scene appears tranquil, when Joe and Marilyn first landed in Tokyo they were mobbed by fans - to the extent that the couple had to take refuge back in the plane. Joe and Marilyn eventually had to leave via the baggage hatch and hide in the customs hall until the fuss died down a little. However, when they arrived at the Imperial Hotel they were mobbed again and the fans refused to disperse until Marilyn appeared on a balcony to wave.

Opposite: Marilyn arrives at Seoul City Airport by chopper, on her way to entertain the American troops who were still stationed in war-torn Korea. She had been invited by the Far East command of General John E. Hull.

In Korea...

Opposite: Despite the sub-zero temperatures and occasional flurries of snow, Marilyn appeared in a low-cut, skin-tight purple sequined gown - with no underwear. At the time she did not appear to notice the cold but she was to suffer for it later, coming down with pneumonia after she had returned to Japan. Here her famous wiggle is demonstrated to appreciative troops, who answered with whistles, cat calls and applause.

Above: Sergeant Guy Morgan, from Marion, North Carolina, presents Marilyn with a 25th Division "Wolfhounds" scarf.

Right: During the four-day tour, Marilyn did ten shows, singing such favorites as "Diamonds Are a Girl's Best Friend", "Bye Bye Baby" and "Somebody to Love Me". She also included "Do It Again", but the lyrics had to be toned down to "kiss me again" to avoid inflaming the over-excited audience any further. Here she is on stage at the K-47 airbase in Chunchon, Korea.

Above: Many of the soldiers who had come to see Marilyn had walked for over ten miles and they gave her a rapturous welcome. While she was in Korea, many of her performances were filmed and the footage was later put together to create a documentary, which she narrated.

Opposite above: Pfc. James R. Goggin gets a bit of personal service, as Marilyn helps out in the 2nd Division Mess.

Opposite below: Marilyn samples the food herself. Later soldiers said that her appetite was "Great, she eats everything".

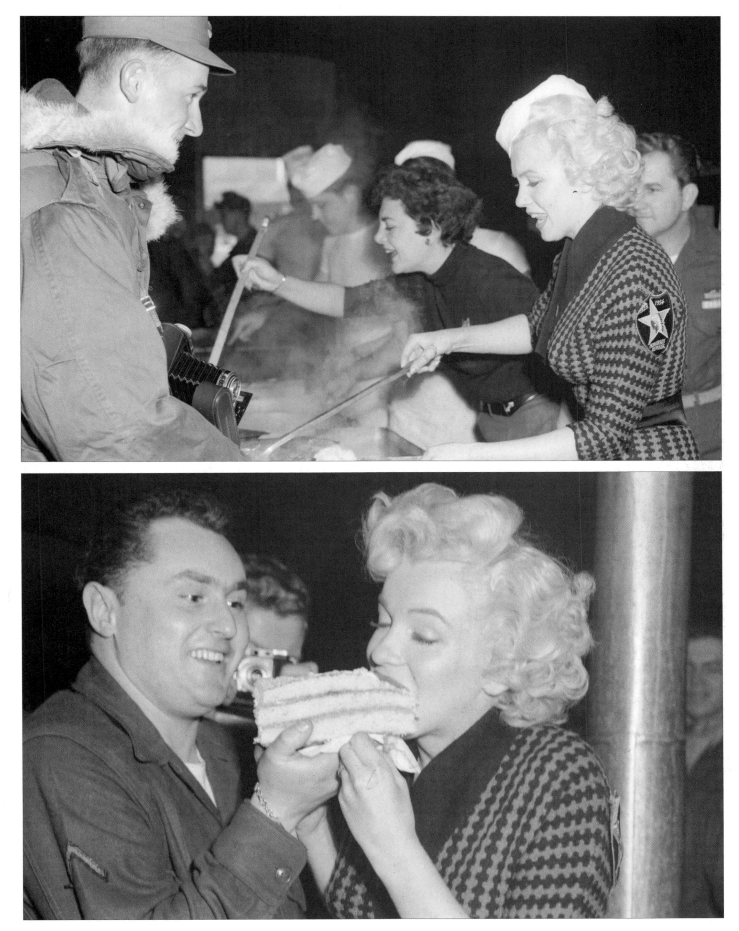

Geisha Girls

Left: After a sukiyaki dinner in Kobe, Japan, Marilyn poses with a group of Geisha girls. The dinner had been given in honor of Joe DiMaggio by the Central League, one of Japan's professional baseball organizations, but as usual it was Marilyn who was the centre of attention. So soon after their honeymoon, the trip had brought home to Joe how difficult it would be to be married to the world's greatest sex-symbol. He was not comfortable with his wife being admired by other men, and more crucially he disliked the fact that Marilyn encouraged them and enjoyed all the attention.

Below: Marilyn tries out her baseball batting skills.

Opposite: On her return to America, Marilyn felt refreshed and ready to resume her battle for better contract terms. During her absence, Charles Feldman, of Famous Artists, had been working tirelessly on her behalf - although she still had not signed a contract with his agency.

No Joe...

At the *Photoplay* magazine awards in Hollywood in March 1954, Marilyn was pictured with actor Alan Ladd (above) and columnist and friend Sidney Skolsky (opposite). She explained to the Press that Joe did not like crowds - but he came to collect her afterwards. Marilyn had been honored as Most Popular Film Actress of 1953.

Having spent some time with Joe in San Francisco, Marilyn was still under suspension, but had returned to Hollywood for the *Photoplay* awards. The contractual negotiations between the studio and Charles Feldman were protracted but sufficient progress had been made for her to begin work on *There's No Business Like Show Business*. *The Girl in Pink Tights* had been dropped and Fox conceded that Marilyn should not make more than two movies each year. However, she had been refused the level of creative control she sought, only being granted approval of the choreographer and dramatic coach.

Starting a family?

Above: Marilyn demonstrates her singing and dancing skills in *There's No Business Like Show Business*. Her part had been written into the script specially, to give her an alternative project to *The Girl in Pink Tights*.

Left: Marilyn with co-star Johnnie Ray, who played Steve Donahue. His character starts as part of the Donahue song and dance act, but he leaves to become ordained as a priest.

Opposite: Due to her lingering illness throughout filming, Marilyn apparently fainted three times on set, which gave rise to rumors that she was pregnant. She told interested newsmen that she and Joe certainly wanted to start a family, but that she was not yet expecting.

There's no business like show business...

Above: A production still from *There's No Business Like Show Business*. Marilyn's character of Vicky was given some of the production numbers written for Ethel Merman - which led to an interesting mixture of styles. Unlike the other lead actors, Marilyn was not a professional singer or dancer, but she worked hard with her coaches so her performance would measure up. Marilyn's routines were choreographed by Jack Cole with whom she had worked on *Gentlemen Prefer Blondes* but the others were created by Robert Alton.

Opposite: Marilyn with her drama coach, Natasha Lytess, during filming. Marilyn was only to do one further movie with her - *The Seven Year Itch* later in 1954. Natasha had tried to pressure Marilyn into doing *The Girl in Pink Tights*, and Joe DiMaggio disliked her intensely, so by 1956 she had been replaced by Paula Strasberg.

"After You Get What You Want...."

Opposite: The dress Marilyn wore for her performance of Irving Berlin's "After You Get What You Want You Don't Want It" in *There's No Business Like Show Business*, consisted of sequined white net over a flesh-colored body stocking, with strategically-placed silver and white flowers and a slit high up onto the hip, masked with white fringing. Marilyn had recently signed an exclusive recording contract with RCA, so the film soundtrack featured Broadway star Dolores Gray.

Above: Marilyn takes some time out to visit Merle Oberon on the set of her new movie, in which she was playing Napoleon's Josephine, and director Henry Koster entertains them both with a joke.

Left: Lewis K. Gough, past National Commander of the American Legion, presents Marilyn with a trophy and plaque in July 1954, for her morale-building activities on behalf of the armed forces.

Miss Modesty...

Above: Marilyn and Joe having dinner at El Morocco on East 54th Street in New York where Marilyn was on location filming *The Seven Year Itch*. Despite the smiles, Joe was deeply unhappy about his wife's continuing career. He wanted her to settle down and be a wife - and hopefully a mother - but Marilyn was still totally absorbed in her work.

Joe objected strongly to Marilyn's habit of wearing revealing and low-cut dresses and in deference to him she often wore much more modest outfits during their brief marriage (opposite). He also disliked her going without underwear - and once made her wait in the powder room of a restaurant until suitable undergarments could be delivered. Despite these problems Marilyn found him deeply attractive - soon after they met she said of him, "He has the grace and beauty of a Michelangelo. He moves like a living statue."

Right: The strategically placed fabric rose was no doubt there to appease Joe - and photographers did have a habit of shooting from above when Marilyn wore low-cut dresses.

The Seven Year Itch

Above: Backstage at the Martin Beck Theater, Marilyn has her eyes made up Oriental-style by actor David Wayne, as Joe looks on, amused. The two of them had been to see *The Teahouse of the August Moon*, in which Wayne starred.

Opposite: Marilyn listens to director Billy Wilder outside the apartment on East 61st where some of the exterior sequences of *The Seven Year Itch* were filmed. Wilder had seen George Axelrod's adult comedy after it opened on Broadway in 1952 and had recognized its potential for adaptation for the cinema, although Hollywood's Production Code meant that the screenplay had to be less daring than the original production. While Marilyn had agreed to begin work on *There's No Business Like Show Business*, her agent, Charles Feldman, had been involved in securing the role of "The Girl"- the archetypal dumb blonde without even a name - for Marilyn.

The story is slight: husband Richard Sherman (Tom Ewell) is alone in New York during a sweltering summer, as his wife and young son have left for Maine. Sherman is determined to work, but is distracted by the arrival of "The Girl" (Marilyn), who has sublet one of his neighbor's apartments. Because of the heat, she walks around her apartment scantily dressed and keeps her "undies" in the icebox. He fantasizes about starting a relationship with her but she is more interested in his air-conditioned apartment - and is relieved to find that he is a married man so she feels safe with him!

Left: At the end of the picture, Sherman decides on fidelity and goes off, taking his son's canoe paddle, to join his wife and son, leaving Marilyn with the use of both the apartments.

Below: During one of the movie's fantasy sequences "The Girl" gets her toe caught in the faucet and has to be freed by a plumber, played by Victor Moore.

Opposite: The heat wave that is an integral part of the plot was also an excuse for Marilyn to wear all kinds of skimpy costumes.

Every male fantasy...

Philip Strassberg of the *New York Daily Mirror* said of *The Seven Year Itch*, "This is the film that every red-blooded American male has been awaiting ever since the publication of the tease photos showing the wind lifting Marilyn Monroe's skirt above her shapely gams. It was worth waiting for."

However, much the footage taken on location on Lexington Avenue and 52nd Street was not used in the movie because of the background noise and poor light. The scene was shot again on a soundstage back at the Fox studio in Hollywood. The famous pleated, white halter-neck dress that Marilyn wore was part of a set of costumes designed by William Travilla, who had worked on Marilyn's costumes for *Gentlemen Prefer Blondes*.

The famous skirt sequence

The shooting of the skirt-lifting scene on the street was as much about publicizing the movie as about getting the scene. The studio publicity department had leaked plans to the Press, so by the time filming started there were hundreds of photographers and thousands of cheering onlookers. At least fifteen takes were done, leading Marilyn to comment to director Billy Wilder that she hoped they weren't for his private collection, to be screened at stag shows. The skirt blew up past Marilyn's waist several times - and even though she wore two pairs of panties the final shots were far too revealing to be used in the movie.

Unfortunately, Joe had been persuaded to come and watch the filming by his friend Walter Winchell. The sight of his wife displaying her underwear as thousands of men cheered was too much for him, and he left the scene looking visibly displeased. Back at the hotel that night he and Marilyn argued badly, and the next day he left New York for California.

Working with Billy Wilder

Opposite: Marilyn discusses a scene with Billy Wilder on the set of *The Seven Year Itch*. Marilyn had been very keen to work with him - although that didn't stop her arriving late and requiring numerous retakes even when Wilder was happy. Wilder said of her later, "She is a very great actress. Better Marilyn late than most of the others on time."Marilyn often had difficulty remembering her lines so Wilder broke down scenes into smaller sequences to aid her. Despite this, the movie was almost two weeks behind schedule on 4 November when principal photography was finished.

Above: Marilyn with Tom Ewell, in a publicity still for the movie. Although Marilyn had been Wilder's first choice to play "The Girl" the role of Sherman had been more difficult to cast. Wilder had been favorably impressed by Walter Matthau's audition and Gary Cooper had also been seriously considered before the part was given to Tom Ewell who had begun his career in theater and had played Sherman in the original Broadway play.

Above: Despite Sherman's fantasies, "The Girl" is entirely innocent and has no idea how he feels about her. Marilyn was superb at putting across a sense of sexuality with no apparent awareness of the effect she was having. Co-star Tom Ewell found her to be charming and courteous in real life - she even apologized for the taste of cough medicine on her breath during their kissing scene. She was taking it for a lung infection caught during the skirt-lifting sequence.

The star and the stand-in...

Above: Marilyn with Billy Wilder and Tom Ewell during filming in New York in September 1954.

Right: Gloria Mosolino, who was Marilyn's stand-in during shooting of *The Seven Year Itch* in New York. Before Marilyn came on set, Gloria had done the skirt-lifting scene eight times to test the lighting and the blower system. She was a professional stand-in, but such essential people in the production process usually stay in the background since they rarely make it into the final movie. Such was Press interest in the sequence, however, that even Gloria was interviewed - and the folks back home in Pottsville, Pennsylvania, were horrified that she had revealed her undies in public for $20 a day and lunch money.

Spot the difference

Opposite: Europe's glamorous screen star Gina Lollobrigida had once said with some emphasis that she and Marilyn were quite different. This prompted Broadway columnist Earl Wilson to bring the two of them together at the Trans-Lux Theater in New York. Despite her view, the resulting picture reveals several similarities...

Above: Back in Hollywood, Marilyn was pictured with her attorney, Jerry Giesler, outside her Beverly Hills home. Newsmen were gathered to hear a statement, as studio publicist Harry Brand had recently announced that Marilyn was filing for divorce from the Yankee Clipper.

Heading for divorce...

Marilyn clings to Jerry Giesler for support as he gives an official statement to the Press on 6 October, 1954, revealing that she had filed a suit for divorce on the grounds of "mental cruelty" against Joe DiMaggio. As Marilyn posed for photographers she was obviously close to tears, and she refused to say a word herself, leaving all the talking to Giesler.

Everyone speculated about what had gone wrong after only nine months of marriage, as to outsiders they had seemed to be such a golden couple. Marilyn later described their marriage as a "sort of crazy, difficult friendship with sexual privileges. Later I learned that's what marriages often are."

Joe moves out

Above: After the Press statement, Marilyn leaves her home in her attorney's car, heading for the studio where she was to complete scenes for *The Seven Year Itch*.

Opposite: Joe had already left the house that morning, moving his possessions out with the help of his friend Reno Barsocchini. He told reporters he was leaving Los Angeles and would not be coming back to the house that he had rented to share with Marilyn, but he refused to discuss the divorce action any further. Privately, he was reluctant to accept the proceedings as final, making several attempts to persuade Marilyn to change her mind.

Divorce granted

Opposite: In court in Santa Monica in California, before Judge Orlando H. Rhodes, Marilyn sat subdued and dressed all in black. She gave ten minutes of tearful testimony, alleging that Joe was "cold and indifferent, would get into moods and wouldn't speak to me for days at a time...if I tried to coax him to talk to me, he wouldn't answer me at all or he would say 'Leave me alone! Stop nagging me!'"

Above: Marilyn puts her signature to her divorce papers. There were tears in her eyes when the judge said, "Divorce granted." However, it was not final until the following year, October 1955.

Marilyn in hospital

Opposite: Marilyn poses for stills at the studio, although she was just about to go into the Cedars of Lebanon Hospital in Los Angeles for surgery to correct her chronic endometriosis.

Right: Although she tried to leave the hospital by the back door on 12 November, 1954, newsmen were lying in wait to catch her looking tired and ill and far from her usual glamorous self. Despite the divorce, Joe practically lived at the hospital during the five days she was there, and visited her constantly at home in the early part of November. This started rumors that a reconciliation was on the cards - but Marilyn denied it.

Above: Newsmen and curious onlookers throng round as Marilyn leaves the Santa Monica Superior Court on 27 October, 1954, followed by her attorney, Jerry Giesler.

What's in the stars?

Above: Marilyn has her palm read by fortune teller Hassan, at the Beverly Hills Hotel. He couldn't have got it more wrong - he said she was an excellent sailor, whereas Marilyn commented that she got seasick just looking at water, and he said she would go on to have two children.

Opposite: Marilyn being interviewed by Maria Romero at the Beverly Hills Hotel, accompanied by photographer Milton Greene who had come to California with ambitions of becoming a movie producer. Marilyn had first met Greene in the spring of 1954 and was delighted to find in him someone who appreciated her talent and supported her desire for more creative control of her material.

Leaving L.A.

For once Marilyn keeps her curves well covered as she chats with Charlie Farrell at the Racquet Club in Palm Springs in December 1954. She was soon to leave for New York, where she was to remain for the whole of the following year - except for a brief trip back in early January 1955 to film additional dialogue for *The Seven Year Itch*.

After consultations with a lawyer over her contract with Fox, Marilyn sacked her agent Charlie Feldman and announced that she and Greene had established their own company, Marilyn Monroe Productions.

New look Marilyn?

At a Press conference to launch Marilyn Monroe Productions in January 1955 in New York, reporters were told to expect a "new and different" Marilyn, so they were rather disappointed when she appeared looking very much like the old model. She had bleached her hair a more platinum blonde and was dressed all in white, with a pure white mink, in an effort to look like Jean Harlow, as the first movie the new company intended to produce was Harlow's life story, with Marilyn in the lead role. The effect was rather lost on the assembled members of the Press, who seemed more interested in whether the mink actually belonged to Marilyn; she replied, "It's mine for the night."

Just visiting

Opposite: Milton Greene and Marilyn had become sidetracked by the idea of portraying her as the ideal person to play Harlow, and the result was disastrous. The newspaper coverage the following day didn't even mention the formation of Marilyn Monroe Productions, instead being full of jokey comments, such as, "The new her didn't show up."

Left and above: Despite her estrangement from Twentieth Century Fox, Marilyn returned to Hollywood to reshoot one scene for *The Seven Year Itch*. Pausing on the staircase of the set, dressed in a nightgown and high-heeled slippers, she only had one line to say: "We can do this all summer." Afterwards she told newsmen that she hoped she could work out her differences with the studio and quipped that she was a changed woman - and might even start wearing underwear.

Above: Marilyn with Joe DiMaggio, Joe's brother Dominic, and Dominic's wife, leaving a restaurant in Boston. Newsmen wanted to know if the meeting was a reconciliation, but Marilyn assured them it was not.

Left: While she was living in New York, Marilyn was involved in several campaigns to raise money for charity. Here she gives the Press advance warning of the date of her appearance on the opening night of the circus, in aid of the New York Arthritis and Rheumatism Foundation.

Opposite: Publicity shot for *The Seven Year Itch*, which was soon to be released. At a party shortly after shooting finished, director Billy Wilder told Marilyn to stay with the character she had created, and to stop trying to move into more serious acting roles. Although she respected Wilder as a director, Marilyn had no intention of taking his advice.

A new career?

Marilyn hands a program to a rather surprised-looking Milton Berle (above), at the New York première of *East of Eden*, which starred James Dean. She was acting as a celebrity usherette in the Astor Theater, and the proceeds from the occasion were donated to the Actors Studio by director Elia Kazan.

Marilyn had recently become involved with the Actors' Studio, both attending sessions there and privately studying drama with Lee Strasberg at his home. Although Strasberg was not impressed with the world of film, feeling that stage acting was the only true medium, he was quick to use Marilyn's celebrity to earn additional money for the Studio and for himself personally. In Strasberg Marilyn felt she had found someone who understood her needs and could offer her the opportunity to become a serious actress. She had conquered Hollywood but still craved the respect that she had imagined would come with stardom.

A social success

Left: Marilyn takes the floor with Truman Capote at El Morocco in 1955 - but seems rather distracted by something across the room. She and Capote had first met in 1950 and they became friends. He wanted Marilyn to play Holly Golightly in *Breakfast at Tiffany's*, but the part finally went to Audrey Hepburn - who was nominated for an Oscar as Best Actress in the role.

Opposite: At the opening night of Tennessee Williams' play, *Cat on a Hot Tin Roof*, Marilyn caught everyone's attention in a skin-tight sheath dress and a white mink. In New York Marilyn had an opportunity to change her life. She had been taken up by the literary set and was in great social demand. It was only a matter of time before she was to renew her aquaintance with Arthur Miller.

Below: Milton Berle, acting as the ringmaster of the Barnum & Bailey circus, gets an armful of Monroe charms at a rehearsal for her forthcoming appearance in aid of charity.

Pink elephant...

Left : At the opening of the Ringling Brothers Barnum & Bailey Circus at Madison Square Garden in New York at the end of March 1955, Marilyn led the parade mounted on a pink elephant to portray "The Day After New Year's Eve" or a "Pleasant Hangover". The crowd of 18,000, who had paid $50 per ticket, roared with approval when she appeared.

Below: The week-long Bement Centennial celebrations included a beard-growing contest - and Marilyn was invited to test the authenticity of some of the entrants' facial hair.

Although she continued to make some celebrity appearances, Marilyn settled to a routine in New York. She attended the Actors Studio regularly, saw her analyst almost daily and visited the Strasbergs at home frequently. She had also begun to see Arthur Miller, taking great care to avoid the attention of the Press.

Dripping with jewels...

Left: Looking every inch the movie star, Marilyn appears at an event for the Jewelers' Association in New York, dressed in a costume made entirely of jewellery.

The Seven Year Itch

The June 1955 première of *The Seven Year Itch* was a gala affair, with stars such as Grace Kelly, Henry Fonda, Eddie Fisher and Richard Rodgers attending. To mark the occasion, a 52-foot high poster of Marilyn, in the famous skirt-lifting pose, was erected above Loew's State Theater in Times Square in New York. The one shown opposite was the second version - the first had to be replaced as there were complaints that it was too revealing. The image turned Marilyn into a vivid cultural icon, which still endures today. Marilyn was accompanied to the première by Joe, sparking rumors of a reconciliation, but she told reporters they were "just good friends". The movie went on to become the biggest hit of that summer, making a fortune for Fox - but Marilyn was still not paid her bonus as agreed.

CHAPTER FOUR

The Prince and the Showgirl

At the beginning of 1956, Twentieth Century Fox issued a Press release saying that they and Marilyn had finally come to terms, and that she would soon return to Hollywood. Many people had not really expected her to win and the victory made certain areas of the Press begin to sit up and take notice of the "new" Marilyn - *Time* magazine even called her a "shrewd businesswoman". As if she felt that now she had reached a turning point, soon she legally changed her name to Marilyn Monroe.

Meanwhile, she stayed in New York, continuing her acting classes with Strasberg. Although she had been both studying and attending sessions she was not a member of the Actors Studio, which involved a formal audition and official approval. Once accepted, members were free to perform as little or as much as they liked. However, in February, Marilyn acted at the Studio in front of a proper audience for the first time, after Strasberg convinced her that she was ready. The scene chosen was the introductory one from *Anna Christie*, where Anna appears in a bar on her return home. It had already been made famous by Greta Garbo, since it was the opening scene in the Swedish star's first talking picture, and so became forever linked with the "Garbo talks!"advertisements. Before she went on, Marilyn was almost paralyzed with nerves, but once she began she performed perfectly, without forgetting any of her lines. Most people in the audience were astonished at the depth of her interpretation, and at the end they applauded - although it wasn't usual to do so at Studio sessions. Strasberg was delighted and told her she was a great new

talent - which was exactly what she had been working so hard to achieve. Marilyn was euphoric, but as usual - however well she had done - her delight never lasted, and self-doubt would soon gradually and insidiously return.

An important part of the new contract with Fox was that Marilyn would be able to make one independent movie a year. She fully intended to take advantage of this concession, and she had already begun talks with playwright Terence Rattigan and Laurence Olivier, with a view to appearing in a movie of *The Sleeping Prince,* which Olivier had performed on stage in London with his wife, Vivien Leigh, in 1953. Marilyn wanted to act with Olivier because she felt his reputation as one of the greatest English classical actors would finally make people regard her seriously as a performer. Olivier was keen to do the project because it would give him the opportunity to both co-produce and direct, and he hoped an association with Marilyn would revitalize his career. At a Press conference in New York they announced their plans - but Marilyn upstaged everyone when the narrow strap on her dress broke, threatening to reveal more than was decent. Whether it was by accident or design, it immediately put the old, seductive Marilyn back on center stage, replacing the new, serious one. Perhaps it was deliberate, since she did not yet have confidence in herself as a serious performer, but she had ample evidence that her sex appeal was a powerful weapon that would bring her what she wanted.

At the end of February, Marilyn returned to Hollywood. There they were to find her very much changed - she had taken on the system and won, she had learned self-possession and she certainly appeared much more self-confident. If she thought the events of the last year would bring her respect in the movie world, however, she soon found she was mistaken. Many saw her actions as evidence that she had tried to turn her back on Hollywood, which had put her where she was, while her interest in serious acting was regarded by her detractors as pretension, and not as a performer beginning to grow.

As soon as she arrived back, Natasha Lytess tried to get in touch. In Marilyn's absence, Natasha had been kept on the payroll at Fox, and she expected to step straight back into her old position. However, Strasberg had sent his wife, Paula, to work with Marilyn instead, so Fox abruptly terminated Natasha's employment. Distraught and angry, she immediately tried to contact her former pupil, but she found that her notes were not answered and phone calls were not taken. Finally, in desperation, Natasha turned up at Marilyn's home. She was turned away at the door, but thought she saw Marilyn at the window above. Soon afterwards, she poured out her heart to the Press, claiming that she had "created" Marilyn, and that she deserved better treatment. Natasha's presence had often caused dissension on set, and on later pictures others suspected that - rather than helping - she had fed Marilyn's insecurity by demanding retakes when they were not necessary. She had earned a good living for many years as Marilyn's personal coach, not to mention the many times that her pupil had helped her out financially. Marilyn may have needed Natasha, but the reverse was also true. When it came down to it, Marilyn becoming self-confident enough to be able to function without her was not really in Natasha's interest. Unfortunately for her, Marilyn believed that she had been let down, and she had no hesitation in dropping her former coach, now that she had an acceptable alternative.

Marilyn had returned to start work on *Bus Stop*, movie version of a Broadway hit. The plot was simple - innocent cowboy comes to town and falls in love with bar room singer, regarding her as an "angel" and refusing to accept her tainted past. Singer does not take him seriously,

but is finally won over by his adoration and honest, straightforward character - cue happy ending. This was the first movie that Marilyn was to undertake at Fox after achieving her newly won power, and studio bosses were worried about what impossible demands she might make. When she first saw the elaborate costumes that had been designed for her role, she dismissed them as totally unsuitable, and everyone immediately feared the worst. To their surprise, Marilyn suggested that they should look round the costume department, and she picked out a series of shabby, second-hand outfits that she felt were more appropriate for a down-at-heel bar room girl. Director Joshua Logan was delighted - he had been reluctant to take the project initially, as he had believed that Marilyn couldn't act. He was convinced otherwise by speaking to Strasberg, who had given her a glowing testimony, and now here was evidence that Marilyn really was taking her role seriously. Alone of all her directors, he planned alternative shooting schedules to allow for the occasions when Marilyn was late, which cut down tension on the set considerably.

However, this amicable relationship with her director was not mirrored with Marilyn's co-stars, Don Murray and Hope Lange. Marilyn was annoyed that Murray was impervious to her charms, seeming more interested in Lange - whom he later married. As for Lange, Marilyn insisted that her blonde hair be dyed darker, so as not to compete with her own bright tresses; one of the downsides of Marilyn's new-found power was that her ever-present insecurity could be allowed free rein.

Despite this, Marilyn worked hard, first on location in the desert near Phoenix, Arizona, and then in the mountains at Sun Valley, Idaho. The difference in temperature, coupled with the light clothes she wore in character, brought her down with such a severe case of bronchitis that she had to be hospitalized. Marilyn suffered from recurring bronchial problems, and this was not the first time that she had been so ill that she needed medical attention. She was kept in hospital for four days before she was allowed back to work.

Previous page: A rather sleepy-looking Marilyn arrives at New York's Idlewild Airport early on the morning of 2 June, 1956 - the day after her 30th birthday - after flying in from Los Angeles.

Opposite: Reporters waited outside Marilyn's New York apartment to catch a picture of her after Arthur Miller announced that they were to marry, during his testimony to the House UnAmerican Activities Committee in Washington. She had been keeping out of sight until that moment, having been warned by everyone - including Miller himself - to keep out of his passport problems.

On her return, she faced one of the most important scenes of the movie - Cherie's monologue about her life. Marilyn was renowned for being unable to remember lines, and this was a long speech. Logan knew she would not be able to do it in one take, which raised a second problem - the time she needed to psych herself up to perform. He resolved both problems by keeping the camera running, take after take, without ever calling "Cut!". As he had hoped, Marilyn just kept going, and he was able to piece together all the best bits to create a stunning and moving scene. Marilyn was delighted - Miller had convinced her that she would not be able to consider herself a real performer until she could handle complicated dialogue, and she had finally succeeded.

While filming was in progress, Arthur Miller had been staying in Reno, Nevada, establishing residency so he could obtain a divorce. While they were apart Marilyn kept in touch with long phone calls, but the day after his divorce was finalized they met up in New York. Miller had another problem. He had applied for a passport to go to England, partly to accompany Marilyn when she went to film *The Sleeping Prince*, and also because his play, *A View from the Bridge*, was about to be staged there. However, he had been briefly associated with the Communist Party many years before, and had already been turned down for a passport on a previous occasion - and it was now the height of the McCarthy witch-hunts against Communism. He was called to appear before the House UnAmerican Activities Committee to testify, and he co-operated fully - except that he refused to name names. Despite this, he was at first not held in contempt, as many others taking a similar stance had

Opposite: According to studio publicity, Marilyn's vital statistics were 38-23-36 and she was 5'5" tall. She was certainly more voluptuous than many of today's female stars, but curves were much more fashionable in the fifties.

Above: Arthur Miller and Marilyn pose for photographers with Laurence Olivier just after their arrival in England.

been - to some extent because everyone was distracted by his announcement that he intended to marry Marilyn.

As the news of the impending nuptials spread, the Press went crazy. Newsmen and photographers camped outside their door, and followed them everywhere they went, even after they left New York for the Miller family home at Roxbury, Connecticut. Marilyn was used to such attention, but Miller was not. He was also not the kind of writer who could work in any surroundings, and in these conditions he found it impossible to produce the rewrites he was under a deadline to complete. Finally they married in secret, in a judge's chambers just over the state line in White Plains, New York, followed by a Jewish ceremony, also in secret, in New York. After the event was officially announced, Miller hoped that everyone could go back to normal life. Little did he know that his life with Marilyn would never be normal.

Two weeks later, after Miller finally obtained his passport he and Marilyn arrived in England. *The Sleeping Prince* was to be filmed as *The Prince and the Showgirl*, but the project was not a good experience for most of those concerned. The first problem had come up before they even left America - Strasberg demanded that his wife, Paula, be paid a guaranteed salary of $25,000 for ten weeks' work plus expenses - far more than anyone else on the picture except Olivier and Marilyn herself. When Milton Greene, Marilyn's business partner, understandably objected to this, Strasberg simply pointed out how fragile Marilyn was, and said that he would accept a percentage of the movie's profits instead. Apart from using her to improve his financial situation, many believe that Strasberg also manipulated her for his own ends. Marilyn was his most high-profile pupil, and he was seemingly determined that he alone would get the credit for her achievements. Far from really supporting her on *The Prince and the Showgirl*, he constantly criticized Olivier - who regarded Method acting with contempt - in long telephone calls from New York, while Olivier's direction of Marilyn was undermined by Paula Strasberg on set. However, Strasberg was careful not to get involved personally in the movie - so if Marilyn succeeded he could take the credit, while if she failed he could blame Olivier.

As for Olivier himself, apart from his problems with Paula Strasberg he was exasperated by Marilyn's lateness and difficulty in remembering lines, and was frustrated by his inability to get through to her. Marilyn had been excited about working with such a famous and respected actor, but now she was afraid he would ruin her performance. She thought he was condescending much of the time - particularly after he told her before one scene to "be sexy". For her, the movie had never been about "being sexy" - it was about being accepted as a serious performer. In this she had misjudged the material, because in fact the role called for exactly the kind of beautiful, uncomplicated and seductive blonde that she had played so well so many times in the past.

On top of all this, Marilyn and Miller's marriage was already in some trouble - it was the first time the two of them had spent extended time together, and the first time Miller had had to deal at first-hand with her work anxieties, sleeplessness and insecurity. Marilyn the person had turned out to be quite different from Marilyn the fantasy. Miller was in the habit of jotting down stray thoughts for use in later work, and apparently Marilyn read

some of them, which had led her to doubt that Miller really did love her. From that moment on, she never felt quite so safe and secure in Miller's love as she had done before. There was further unhappiness in their marriage when towards the end of August, Marilyn became pregnant with a much-wanted child, but miscarried the baby within a few weeks.

Marilyn had also come to distrust her business partner, Milton Greene. Greene and Miller had always disliked and distrusted one another, each resenting the influence the other had on Marilyn. Greene was not happy that Miller intended to be actively involved in Marilyn Monroe Productions. In turn, Miller had no faith in Greene's abilities, and he tried to convince Marilyn that she didn't need him. As for Marilyn herself, she came to suspect that Greene was working against her, not supporting her in arguments with others on set and going along with cuts of her scenes. All in all, it was a miracle that *The Prince and the Showgirl* came in under budget and more or less on time.

Below: Marilyn and Arthur attend the opening night of *A View from the Bridge* in London.

The Prince and the Showgirl...

At a Press conference at the Plaza Hotel in New York in February 1956, Marilyn and Laurence Olivier announced their intention to make a version of Terence Rattigan's *The Sleeping Prince*. They planned to film in England, where Olivier had had a hit on the London stage with the original play, in which he had starred with his wife, Vivien Leigh. Marilyn had agreed to pay $125,000 for the movie rights and an additional sum for Rattigan to write the screenplay.

The proposed movie about Jean Harlow's life story had fallen through and so this was to be the first project undertaken by Marilyn Monroe Productions.

Above: Marilyn leans forward to speak to eager reporters, telling them, "I'd like to continue my growth in every way possible."

Opposite: Although she looked quite demure in her outfit, complete with coat, scarf and gloves, during the course of the interview the spaghetti strap of Marilyn's dress broke, instantly drawing everyone's attention. Olivier was convinced it had been done on purpose, but it certainly guaranteed that they were both front-page news the following day.

Right: At the end of February 1956, Marilyn poses for photographers as she boards a plane in New York to return to Hollywood. She had been away from the film capital of America for over a year, as negotiations were carried out to resolve her contract dispute with Fox. Most people had felt she would not win her battle with the studio, but now she was returning in triumph having obtained several concessions that were unique at the time - including a percentage of the profits, and approval of script, director and cinematographer.

Previous page: Marilyn and Susan Strasberg, daughter of Marilyn's mentor Lee Strasberg, seem mesmerized by Laurence Olivier. The three were backstage at the Cort Theater in New York, where Susan was appearing in *The Diary of Anne Frank*.

Left: Despite what reporters might have said, there was no denying that Marilyn looked both seriously smart and glamorous in her new wardrobe of tailored suits and matching gloves.

Above: Both Marilyn and Jack Warner look delighted as it is announced that she is to co-star with Laurence Olivier in the movie of *The Sleeping Prince* for Warner Brothers.

Fined!

Left: Marilyn appears in court in Beverly Hills, charged with driving without a license. The offence had taken place back in 1954 when she was first becoming famous, but the judge was not impressed and lectured her severely before imposing a $56 fine.

Opposite: In court, awaiting her turn before the bench, with attorney, Irving L. Stein.

Below: Milton Greene, vice-president of Marilyn's independent production company, faces the Press with her just after she returned to Hollywood following her long exile in New York. Marilyn Monroe Productions and Fox had recently come to terms, so Marilyn had returned in triumph.

Top of the world!

Above: Marilyn chats to James Cagney at a cocktail party given by *Look* magazine in Beverly Hills in March 1956. The Hollywood Press was full of stories about her return to the fold and news of her latest project.

Opposite: The first movie she was scheduled to make for Fox was *Bus Stop*, which was based on a Broadway hit written by William Inge. When the play was adapted for the screen, writer George Axelrod bore Marilyn in mind and added details from her own life. Joshua Logan, who was on the list of 16 directors approved by Marilyn, was well-versed in Stanislavsky and The Method and had a reputation as a talented director of sensitive actors.

Bus Stop

Marilyn plays Cherie, a down-at-heel bar room singer, with Don Murray as Bo Decker, her devoted admirer. While singing "That Old Black Magic" badly in a bar, Cherie is spotted by innocent cowboy Bo, who is in town for a rodeo. He decides to marry her, despite her dubious past, and carry her off to his isolated farm in Montana. At first Cherie will not agree, but eventually she warms to his honest intentions and enthusiasm. On set Don Murray did not always find it easy to work with Marilyn. While shooting the scene where Cherie tries to leave Bo, one of Marilyn's improvised gestures cut Murray's eyelid but Marilyn failed to apologize.

Marilyn vetoed the elaborate costumes originally designed for the part, and picked out some tattered clothes from the studio wardrobe instead, which she felt would be more in keeping with her character. Much of the look of the movie was designed by Milton Greene, who had a wonderful visual eye for what would work on camera.

Above: Hope Lange, making her debut, appeared with Marilyn in *Bus Stop* as a young girl who Cherie meets on the bus. Marilyn insisted that her co-star's hair was tinted a darker shade, so it would not compete with her own blonde looks. Much of Marilyn's dramatic monologue on the bus, in which she told the story of Cherie's life, was cut when the studio insisted the movie was too long - and Marilyn always believed that this had cost her the chance of an Oscar.

Although Logan was patient and tried to accommodate Marilyn's needs, he had a tough time keeping the production on schedule. As before, she found it difficult to remember her lines and spent hours in her dressing room before being able to face the camera. Paula Strasberg had replaced Natasha Lytess as Marilyn's acting coach but although Logan liked her on a personal level, he was not about to have his authority on set undermined and at first confined her to Marilyn's dressing room.

Opposite: Marilyn with Arthur O'Connell, who played Virgil Blassing, the young cowboy's older and wiser guardian.

Mr President...

Opposite: At a party thrown by Joshua Logan, director of *Bus Stop*, Marilyn was introduced to Indonesian President Sukarno. He had particularly asked to meet her because he was interested in Hollywood and her movies were very popular in his country. The party also marked Marilyn's 30th birthday.

Above: At a Press conference, the journalists may all have their heads down but Marilyn - as usual - knows exactly where the camera is.

Right: A kiss for the photographer. Marilyn was far better with stills photographers than she was on a film set - she didn't feel the same pressure to perform, but was still able to conjure up her star persona for the camera. By the time work on *Bus Stop* had finished at the end of May 1956 she was physically and emotionally exhausted. Marilyn had felt the need to show her year with Strasberg had made a difference to her performance and, in addition to this, filming in the desert of Arizona and the cold in Sun Valley had put a strain on her health.

Happy birthday...

Arriving on 2 June at Idlewild Airport in New York on a flight from the west coast, Marilyn is presented with a birthday cake in her limousine. She had celebrated her 30th birthday the previous day in Hollywood. Reporters wanted to know about her romance with playwright Arthur Miller, but she just smiled mysteriously and blew them a kiss.

Mrs Arthur Miller

While Marilyn had been filming *Bus Stop*, Miller had spent some six weeks in Nevada in order to obtain his divorce. He had been called to appear before the House UnAmerican Activities Committee to answer questions about his past association with the Communist Party and had revealed to the Committee that he wanted a passport so he could go to England to "be there with the woman who will then be my wife". Washington reporters descended upon him and he told them that he expected to marry Marilyn within "a day or two", adding that whether or not he got his passport, Marilyn would be going to London as Mrs Arthur Miller.

Reporters then rushed to the apartment on Sutton Place, where Marilyn had been keeping out of sight, to ask for her side of the story. Until then she had refused to be interviewed, afraid of saying the wrong thing and damaging Miller's chances, but now she called an impromptu Press conference and told reporters how happy she was to be getting married.

Two lovebirds...

On 22 June, 1956 Marilyn and Arthur Miller appeared before the Press together in front of the Sutton Place apartment, where they were staying in New York, to talk about their forthcoming wedding. They told reporters they planned a simple ceremony, they had not yet set the date, but that it would be "sometime in July". At one point Marilyn hugged Miller so hard that he had to tell her to stop, "or I'll fall over". Following comments by Francis Walter, chairman of the HUAC, reporters asked Miller if he would enjoy his honeymoon in America if he did not get his passport, but Miller pointed out that it would be difficult to do so, as Marilyn was already committed to going to England.

In the country...

It soon became apparent that reporters would give them no peace, so the happy couple left for Miller's home in Roxbury, Connecticut. Unfortunately the Press soon followed them there. To try to keep them at bay, a photocall was arranged and Miller and Marilyn appeared, casually dressed. They told reporters that there would be no wedding for several days, and Miller appealed to them to go away for a short while and allow Marilyn to get some rest. He promised an announcement the following Friday.

Waiting for news

Opposite: Miller and Marilyn with Miller's basset hound, Hugo. Since they were followed everywhere by newsmen, Miller's cousin, Morty, had carried out some of the wedding preparations on their behalf, including arranging for their blood samples to be tested - which had to be done before they could apply for a license. Details were still secret, but the wedding was planned for 1 July, at the home of Miller's agent, Kay Brown, just over the state border in South Salem, New York and the ceremony was to be performed by Rabbi Robert Goldberg.

Left: While reporters waited for news of the wedding, Miller was waiting for news from the HUAC. Finally, instead of citing Miller for contempt, they gave him until 7 July - six days before Marilyn was scheduled to leave for England - to change his mind and reveal the names of his friends who had attended a Communist-sponsored meeting of authors in the late forties.

A bad omen

Opposite top: Marilyn rushes past reporters, ashen-faced and shaking, after witnessing a terrible accident nearby. Journalist Mara Scherbatoff had been following them in an automobile driven by the young brother of her photographer, who had lost control and crashed into a tree. The boy had some injuries, but Scherbatoff was seriously hurt and she later died in hospital. Miller had had enough of the media circus, and he brought the wedding forward to that evening, arranging for the ceremony to be held at the Westchester County Court House in White Plains, New York, with Judge Seymour Robinowitz officiating.

Above and opposite below: The day after the civil ceremony, the newlyweds looked happy and carefree as they left for a romantic picnic together - although Marilyn privately believed that the death on the very day of her wedding was a bad omen.

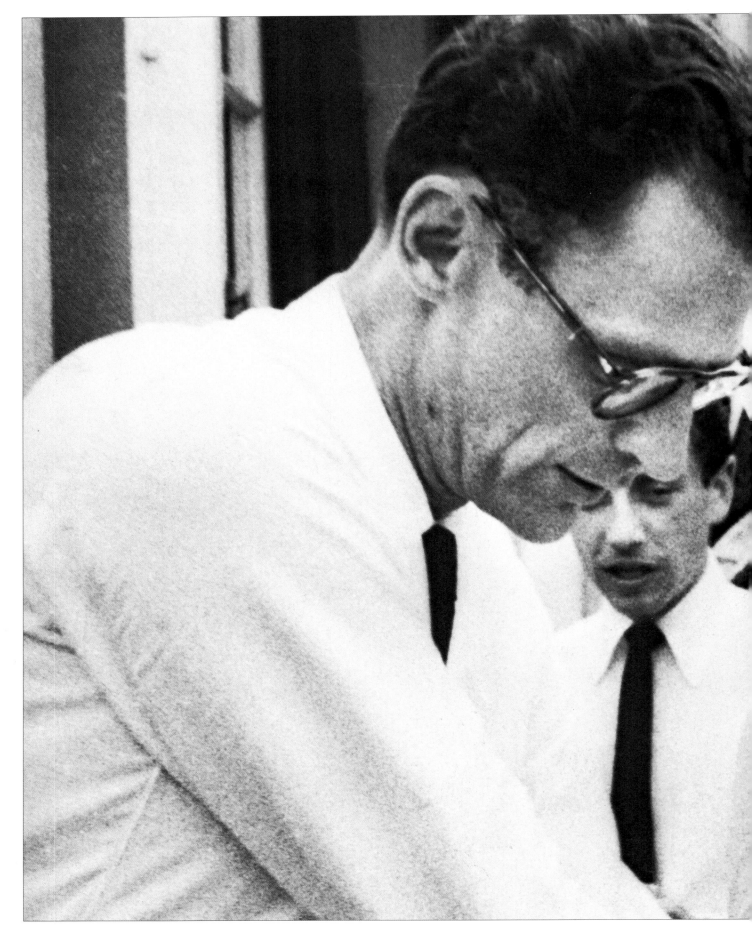

Egghead weds Hourglass

The religious ceremony was held, as planned, in the garden of Kay Brown's farmhouse. The civil ceremony had thrown reporters off guard, so the occasion was only for family and friends. The bride wore a sheath of champagne satin and chiffon, with a scoop neck, and was given away by Lee Strasberg, who she now regarded as a substitute father figure.

London bound

Luckily Miller was granted a passport, and only twelve days after their wedding he and Marilyn were off to London on their honeymoon. Newsmen commented that Marilyn seemed to be a changed woman - for once she was on time for the flight, and she demurely refused to kiss her new husband for the cameras until he patted her on the hand and gave his permission.

Opposite: The long flight from America had left Marilyn looking rather disheveled, but she and Arthur Miller posed happily for London photographers. A Press conference had been arranged at one of the airport hotels, and Marilyn smiled radiantly, proud to be standing with her new husband, and to be embarking on her first movie with her own production company.

Above: Both Laurence Olivier and his wife, Vivien Leigh, had come to the airport to meet the Millers. News had broken in the papers only a couple of days previously that Vivien was pregnant, at the age of forty-two.

Left: Although the trip to England had been organized around Marilyn's filming schedule, it was also the first time the couple had been away together since their marriage and they planned to enjoy some romantic time together.

Next door to the Queen...

A limousine took the Millers to Surrey, along with Milton Greene, while the Oliviers followed in a second car. A grand Georgian mansion, Parkside House, had been rented for Marilyn and Arthur Miller to stay in. It was situated right next to Windsor Great Park - with a private gate into the park itself. A long drive ensured some privacy, but Marilyn insisted that a group of photographers were allowed up to the house immediately, and that they should all pose for a few more pictures - even though a proper Press conference had been scheduled for the following day. Although Vivien Leigh smiled bravely, she was clearly somewhat unhappy at being asked to pose next to a woman twelve years her junior, who was renowned for her attractiveness to men, particularly as the Oliviers' marriage had been going through a rocky patch of late.

Another day, another Press conference

Opposite: Marilyn was delighted that Miller was apparently willing to support her publicly as she geared herself up to begin work. Unfortunately he had never seen this side of her, and it wasn't long before he began to wonder just what he had taken on.

Above and left: Despite a promise to Olivier, Marilyn arrived over an hour late for a Press conference that had been arranged in the Lancaster Room of the Savoy Hotel in London. Olivier had entertained journalists alone while they all waited, and he was not in the best of moods. However, as usual, Marilyn charmed everyone into forgiving her. Previously Olivier had said that he had planned to fall "most shatteringly in love" with Marilyn, but now she was married to Arthur Miller, and he and Vivien were expecting a child together - which might signal a new start in their troubled marriage. He therefore was far more reserved with Marilyn than he had been in New York, which she found very unsettling.

Above: After three Press conferences in three days, Marilyn still managed to look fresh and happy. Photographers were rather disappointed that she was rather conservatively dressed - they had expected someone a bit more like her screen persona. Despite this they enthusiastically snapped her picture, while newsmen screamed questions.

Opposite: To ensure filming went smoothly, Olivier intended to work on a closed set - meaning no Press or outside visitors would be allowed in during shooting - so photographers made the most of every opportunity to take pictures of Marilyn, even catching her with cigarette in hand.

In London...

Above: Interest in Marilyn was at fever pitch in London, and crowds turned out to see her whenever she appeared in public. Despite the fact that this was often very intrusive, she was always aware that she owed her fans a great deal.

Left: For once, Marilyn is not the center of attention. If she chose not to turn on her Marilyn persona, she could often pass unnoticed in a crowd. Despite this, when she and Arthur Miller went to the theater - which they did quite often in London - the number of people who turned out to see them was so great that the police had to be called to clear a path for them to enter and leave the building. Marilyn was used to this kind of public furore, but Miller found it very hard to adapt to it.

Opposite: Olivier and Marilyn share a quiet word at yet another Press conference. They apparently got on famously at these affairs, complimenting each other and appearing to enjoy working together, but unfortunately this happy atmosphere was not destined to last long once filming began.

Following pages: Although they were seemingly enjoying a carefree time in London, both Marilyn and her husband were aware that Congress was about to vote on whether to cite Miller for contempt. Although he had his passport, his problems with the HUAC had not gone away by any means.

The Prince and the Showgirl

Right: Olivier was not only starring as the Grand Duke who falls in love with a showgirl, he was also directing the movie. The working title was still that of the play - *The Sleeping Prince* - but the picture was finally released as *The Prince and the Showgirl*, perhaps to reflect Marilyn's equal billing.

Marilyn quickly gained the support of one of her co-stars - Dame Sybil Thorndike, a legendary actress on the London stage. After less than a week on set, she said to Laurence Olivier, who was an old friend of hers, "You did well in that scene, Larry, but with Marilyn up there, nobody will be watching you. Her manner and timing are just too delicious. And don't be too hard about her tardiness, dear boy. We need her desperately. She's really the only one of us who knows how to act in front of a camera!"

Her remarks did not go down well with Olivier, who was convinced that he was a master of his craft.

Tension on set

Right: Problems on the set of *The Prince and the Showgirl* began almost at once. Olivier did not believe in Method acting, and Marilyn came to mistrust him, particularly after he instructed her to "be sexy" for one scene. Although he was not present in person, Marilyn's mentor, Lee Strasberg, had sent his wife Paula as Marilyn's drama coach and she took every opportunity to undermine Olivier's direction.

Opposite: Marilyn was unwell during most of filming: fearful of failure in front of the camera, she was using alcohol and prescription drugs to help her cope with her anxieties. However, even when she arrived on set looking disheveled after a sleepless night, the combination of Marilyn's ability to sparkle for the camera and the skill of cinematographer Jack Cardiff, who had worked on *The Red Shoes* and *Black Narcissus*, managed to produce a stunning image.

Below: Lee Strasberg, who offered advice and criticism at a distance during filming.

Above: Arthur Miller was not solely in England to accompany Marilyn - he was also there to work. His play, *A View from the Bridge,* was being performed on the London stage. Here he and actress Mary Ure discuss her role.

Left: Marilyn attended the opening night of the play, supporting her husband in his work as he had supported her. They both knew that her presence would guarantee that the Press would also turn out in force.

Opposite: In *The Prince and the Showgirl* Marilyn played Elsie Marina, an American showgirl, who catches the eye of the Prince Regent of Carpathia, who is in London for the coronation of King George V.

At the Comedy...

The opening night of *A View from the Bridge* was held at the Comedy Theatre, but it was performed before the members of a newly created private theater club - the New Watergate Theatre Club. The Lord Chamberlain had objected to a scene in which one man kissed another on the lips, and had refused to grant the necessary permit for public performance. Both Marilyn and her husband had to become members of the club before they were allowed inside to see the play - even though he was the author. Marilyn had recently been ill, but she was still determined to appear.

Above: Both the Millers obviously enjoyed the performance. The story was of particular personal significance to Miller at the time, as it involves a man's decision to betray his friends, which leads to his destruction.

Opposite: Marilyn signs her application form for membership.

Out on the town...

Above: Vivien Leigh was appearing in *South Sea Bubble*, and Marilyn and Miller went to the Lyric Theatre to see a performance. After the show they walked hand-in-hand through an excited crowd.

Opposite: Towards the end of August 1956, Miller decided to fly back to America for a few days to see his children. The trip was intended to be a secret - the name on his ticket was Mr Stevenson - as there was always a possibility that his return to America would precipitate more problems with the HUAC.

Bad news...

Above: While Miller was away, Marilyn was left alone at Parkside House. Marilyn viewed his departure as another small betrayal, particularly since filming *The Prince and the Showgirl* was not progressing as she had anticipated and the atmosphere on the set was strained. Her intake of barbiturates had increased alarmingly, and she was often not fit to work for days at a time. During this period she discovered she was pregnant, but within a few weeks she had miscarried the baby.

Opposite: The Millers leave the Palace Theatre by the stage door, after seeing Brecht's *Caucasian Chalk Circle* performed in German. This was Marilyn's first night out after recovering from her miscarriage, but it was also the couple's celebration of Miller's return from America. They arrived late and a surprised management ushered them into seats in the stalls.

Opening night...

Opposite: Marilyn and Arthur arrive at the black tie première of *A View from the Bridge*. Marilyn wore a scarlet satin gown so tight around the knees that walking was an achievement. As a result of her attendance the publicity for the play was tremendous, and promoter Binkie Beaumont had signed up over 13,000 members to his hastily formed theater club - pocketing the small membership fee.

Marilyn felt that she had lost some part of Miller's love, and she was now working hard to win it back. She had miscarried their baby and she had read some notes he had jotted down which, she felt, showed he regretted having married her. He found her needs hard to cope with, and her constant demands were interfering with his work as a writer and so he had withdrawn somewhat. There were misunderstandings on both sides - he did not appreciate how much she dreaded being abandoned, and she did not understand that a writer may draw on real life, but is not necessarily expressing how he personally feels in his character's views.

Above: Marilyn arrives at a dressmaker to find an outfit in which to be presented to Queen Elizabeth II at the Royal Command Performance of *The Battle of the River Plate* in London, in October 1956. She went in looking pale and timid, but emerged poised, confident and glittering in a gold dress.

Vivien Leigh, Laurence
Olivier, Marilyn and
Miller take their seats for
the performance. Many
members of the audience
were more interested in
studying Marilyn than
watching the play, but it
proved to be a success
and was well reviewed.

Goodbye London

Opposite: Backstage, Marilyn meets some of the cast of *A View from the Bridge*. At the end of the play she accompanied Miller onto the stage and they took a bow hand in hand.

Above: Goodbye London... Marilyn and her husband were both relieved when filming was over and they were able to return to America. The strain of working had brought out a different side of Marilyn, one that Miller had never had to cope with before. As for Marilyn, she had come to doubt that Miller really loved her. In addition to this, in September Marilyn had been pregnant, but had lost her much-wanted baby within a few weeks.

Kisses

On 20 November, 1956 the Oliviers saw the Millers off at London Airport. It was kisses all round as everyone agreed that they had to put on a good face in public for the sake of the movie. It was not only the Millers who were going home disillusioned - Olivier was disappointed that he had apparently missed an opportunity to revive his flagging career, while Vivien had also lost her baby - and as it turned out, her last chance to save the marriage. She and Marilyn had totally failed to develop any kind of rapport, and during the time in England they had only met on formal occasions.

After his experience on this film, Olivier considered Marilyn a "thoroughly ill-mannered and rude girl", but years later he said, "Maybe I was tetchy with Marilyn and with myself, because I felt my career was in a rut... I was as good as could be, and, Marilyn! Marilyn was quite wonderful, the best of all."

Marilyn visits the Actors Studio on her return to New York, telling reporters that she still longed to do dramatic roles.

Opposite: Proceeds from the premiere of Elia Kazan's *Baby Doll*, starring Carroll Baker, were pledged to the Actors Studio, since many of its stars were members and Kazan was the director. Marilyn was roped in as a celebrity usherette.

CHAPTER FIVE

Some Like It Hot

While Marilyn had been away in England, *Bus Stop* had been released. She had seen a rough cut of the movie in London, and had been devastated because part of her performance had been cut, and much of the dramatic monologue that she was so proud of had ended up on the cutting-room floor. She had wanted Miller and Strasberg to see her achievement, and now they never would. She also felt that the cuts had ruined her chances of an Oscar nomination - and what was all the more galling was that Don Murray was nominated as Best Supporting Actor, and as Most Promising Newcomer for the British Academy Awards. She turned on director Joshua Logan, berating him for spoiling her performance, but in fact he had fought to keep much of the material and been overruled by studio bosses, who felt the movie was too long. Despite this, the reviews were glowing, with almost every newspaper critic commenting that Marilyn had proved that she really could act.

Back in New York at the beginning of 1957, the rough cut of *The Prince and the Showgirl* did not initially look quite as good, and when it was first released later in the year the reviews were mixed. However, it picked up five nominations for the British Academy Awards, including Best Foreign Actress for Marilyn. In the event, she did not win, but in 1959 it did bring her Italy's most prestigious acting award - the David Di Donatello statuette for Best Actress in a Foreign Film. Many critics now regard it as one of her finest performances, and she easily steals the picture from Olivier. However, at the time Marilyn felt

that Milton Greene had let her down with their first independent production, and Miller fueled this view, finally convincing her that she no longer needed Greene. As a result, Greene was fired from Marilyn Monroe Productions and a new board of directors was appointed. He may have made mistakes, but it was a poor return for a man who had practically given up his own career to help Marilyn, who had supported her financially when she was on suspension throughout the greater part of 1955, and who had helped her achieve her revised contract with Fox. Much later, Marilyn confessed to Greene's wife, Amy, that Milton was the only man she had ever trusted, but that Miller had driven him away and she had felt unable to resist. The truth was that at the time, Marilyn was more concerned with making a success of her shaky marriage.

After all the draining experiences in England, she now wanted to take some time off. Her contract with Fox called for her to make four movies for them within seven years, of which she had so far completed one. There were plans for her to appear in a remake of *The Blue Angel*, with Spencer Tracy as co-star, but despite prolonged negotiations on both sides the idea was eventually shelved. Until Fox came up with an acceptable project, she could choose whether to work or not. She decided that what she really wanted to do was to try and be a good wife: to create a proper home for Miller, where he could work in peace, and to have a baby. For the moment she put her own work on hold and concentrated on furnishing their new apartment in New York, complete with a writing room for Miller, while she also began treatment at Doctors Hospital to enable her to carry a baby to term.

Meanwhile, events from the past were coming back to haunt both Miller and Marilyn's ex-husband, Joe DiMaggio. First of all, in February 1957 Miller was finally indicted by a federal grand jury on two counts of contempt of Congress, as a result of his failure to name names at his House UnAmerican Activities Committee hearing in 1956. If he was found guilty, each count could mean a huge fine and up to a year in prison. His lawyers were confident that he would win, because the questions he had refused to answer were actually nothing to do with what the HUAC was supposed to be investigating, namely the abuse of passports. Despite this, Miller was too stressed to concentrate on his work, partly because of the legal proceedings hanging over him, and also because his defense would run up huge legal fees.

As for DiMaggio, an event that had happened in 1954, just after his divorce from Marilyn had been granted, now suddenly and unexpectedly hit the news. After they separated, DiMaggio had hired a private detective to follow Marilyn, and had come to the conclusion that she was having an affair with her voice coach, Hal Schaefer. In early November, DiMaggio and Frank Sinatra were having a drink together when news came that Marilyn's automobile had been seen parked outside an apartment building. DiMaggio and Sinatra joined the detective and his associate outside, and the four of them broke into one of the apartments, expecting to catch Marilyn *in flagrante delecto*. However, they had the wrong apartment - they had broken down the door of Florence Kee. The noise had alerted the rest of the building, so Marilyn, who was apparently having dinner with Schaefer and another woman next door, escaped without being seen. At the time, Sinatra managed to keep his and DiMaggio's name out of the newspapers, but many months later the full story of the event which had become known as the "Wrong Door" raid was published in *Confidential* magazine. Kee promptly sued her famous intruders, but the case dragged on for years, so Sinatra was not called to testify until early 1957. The newspapers had a field day, but eventually DiMaggio settled out of court.

Unfortunately, Miller's legal problems were not to be settled so easily. Marilyn came with him to Washington, although by now she was again pregnant. Reporters swarmed over the Federal District Court to see her, but she was keeping out of sight and Miller explained that he thought that everyone should stay focused on the issue at hand. After that, journalists tried to contact Marilyn at the house where the Millers were staying. Finally she appeared to speak to them, clearly stating her support for her husband. At the end of a six-day hearing, the defendant was found guilty on both counts, though soon afterwards the judge revised his verdict to a conviction on only one charge, for which Miller was fined $500 and received a suspended sentence of one month. His lawyers instantly appealed, and in a much more hopeful mood he and Marilyn left to spend the summer on Long Island.

Their happiness was short-lived - just over two months later Marilyn collapsed in terrible pain and was rushed by ambulance to Doctors Hospital in New York. Her much-wanted pregnancy had turned out to be ectopic, and had to be terminated to save her life. Although she was devastated, she managed to put on a good face for reporters as she left the hospital ten days later. However, apart from the natural sadness of losing her baby, she also felt a failure as a wife because she was not able to give Miller a child, and she now seemed convinced that sooner or later he would leave her. Shortly afterwards, she took an overdose of sleeping pills, but Miller found her and called for help. In an attempt to convince her that he still loved her, he started work on turning his short story, *The Misfits*, into a screenplay for her. Unfortunately, Marilyn did not take this gesture in quite the way in which it was intended. Now that Miller was busy working he cut himself off at the very moment when she needed emotional support, and - what was even worse - she began to suspect that he was only staying with her to get his screenplay accepted and revive his flagging writing career.

At the beginning of 1958, Twentieth Century Fox began to panic that they had let a year go by without

Previous page: A classic glamor shot of Marilyn Monroe, swathed in furs and posed with lips half open and eyes half closed. It was used as the cover picture on the July 1954 issue of *Movie Fan* magazine, not long after Marilyn's marriage to Joe DiMaggio, with the words, "All My Glamor Is For Joe!"

Opposite: Marilyn smiles as she leaves the Lennox Hill Hospital in New York after gynecological surgery in 1959, which was intended to enable her to carry a baby to term.

getting another Marilyn Monroe movie. They had no intention of accepting *The Misfits* as a potential project until Miller's conviction was overturned, and there was no sign in the immediate future of that happening. However, they had nothing else that Marilyn was prepared to consider. Meanwhile, director Billy Wilder sent her the script for *Some Like It Hot*. The story was set in 1929, and involves two musicians, who inadvertently witness the St Valentine's Day Massacre and have to hide from the Mob. They disguise themselves as women and join an all-girl band, led by singer and ukulele player Sugar Kane. Marilyn was initially not interested in the part, because in the film Sugar never realizes that the two "girls" are men, which Marilyn felt was taking the concept of being a "dumb blonde" to a ridiculous extreme. And had she not fought to get away from being cast in dumb blonde roles?

Below: At the première of *The Prince and the Showgirl* at New York's Radio City Music Hall, Marilyn stops to admire one of the elaborately uniformed soldiers on display. Reviews of the movie were mixed at the time, but Marilyn's performance later became regarded as one of her finest.

Opposite: Director Billy Wilder chats to Marilyn in a break during filming for *Some Like It Hot*, on location on the beach at San Diego, California. Marilyn had intially been wary about playing another dumb blonde, but husband Arthur Miller had persuaded her that the story was a sure-fire winner.

Miller, however, pointed out that the script was outstanding, and would be a sure-fire winner. Both her agents and Fox agreed. Even though the picture was to be made by the Mirisch brothers and distributed by United Artists so they wouldn't make a penny from it, Fox felt it was in their interest to get Marilyn back to work - and if the movie was the success everyone thought it would be, it would enhance her value as a Fox property.

Finally, Marilyn gave in and signed the contract. Again Paula Strasberg was hired as dramatic coach. Billy Wilder, having dealt with Natasha Lytess, knew the score. Renowned for his caustic wit, he soon exerted his authority on set and put Paula firmly in her place, although he welcomed her support of Marilyn. He also admired Marilyn's sense of comedy, and was prepared to listen to her ideas with respect. It was apparently her idea to change Sugar's first appearance to establish her kooky nature from the outset, so the train suddenly lets off a puff of steam as she teeters down the platform on her high heels, making her jump and the audience laugh. Despite these good omens, Marilyn was soon arriving late, demanding retakes and forgetting her lines. As well as her old demons, she now had to cope with an increasing intake of prescribed drugs: sleeping pills to get her to sleep, uppers to wake her up, and tranquilizers to calm her down. Wilder said later that the experience of working on the project brought him to the verge of a breakdown - and although the end result turned out to be worth it, at the time he had not believed there would be a final product.

As an added complication, towards the end of shooting, Marilyn again became pregnant. Luckily the most strenuous parts of the movie had already been filmed, but Marilyn took every opportunity to rest in an attempt to carry the baby to term. However, in December she miscarried this baby too - it was her last attempt to become a mother.

In March 1959, Some Like It Hot had its première on Broadway. It was an instant success, both with the critics and at the box office. It not only outgrossed all other movies in the first half of 1959, but also established a box office record for any comedy that remained unbroken for many years. It is fondly regarded as

Marilyn's best picture by many of her fans, and is still shown regularly after more than four decades.

Despite this massive success, 1959 was to be another year when Marilyn made no movies. Fox was aware that, according to her contract, they had to put her in a movie by 14 April, or lose the right to one of the four pictures they were entitled to. She was assigned to Time and Tide, a script based on novels by William Bradford, to be directed by Elia Kazan. She was due to start work on 14 April, but when Kazan came on board he demanded extensive rewrites, so Marilyn was instructed to remain in New York until they needed her - although her salary would be paid from the original start date. Meanwhile, Kazan decided he didn't want to cast Marilyn, but preferred Lee Remick. Fox had failed to notice that Marilyn's contract specified that filming had to start ten weeks from her official start date - which was April 14 - so they were totally surprised to receive notification from her lawyer on 25 June that she was no longer obliged to appear in Time and Tide. What was worse, she wanted payment for the movie, as per the terms of her contract, even though she hadn't worked on it, and was insisting she be released from one of the pictures she owed. The studio's legal department confirmed that all these demands were in accordance with her contract: Fox should have asked for an extension, and had failed to do so. Although the New York office cast around for an excuse to get out of paying, the Hollywood end wanted to avoid another lawsuit. Marilyn was a really hot property after the success of Some Like It Hot, and they now had another project for her. As a result, all her demands were met - yet again Marilyn had taken on the studio and won.

The new movie was The Billionaire, co-starring Gregory Peck and to be directed by George Cukor. At first Marilyn had been excited and happy about it, and she was scheduled to start work in October rehearsing her musical numbers. However, the movie - later renamed Let's Make Love - didn't start full filming until early in 1960. By the start date, Gregory Peck had dropped out after the script was altered to build Marilyn's role, and her new co-star was French sex symbol Yves Montand.

Opposite: Marilyn waves to newsmen as she is driven away. She always made a big effort to be co-operative with the Press and had quickly developed the skill of turning the coverage to her best advantage. She cultivated allies in the Press - notably Sidney Skolsky, who not only wrote favorably about her in his column, but also helped her to write articles that were published under her own name.

Wrong door raid

Right: Frank Sinatra testifies at the 1957 investigation into the famous "Wrong Door" raid, which had been carried out in 1954. He claimed that he had remained in the automobile while Joe DiMaggio, along with private detective Philip Irwin and his associate, broke down the apartment door to see if Marilyn was inside, but his story was contradicted by Irwin, who said that all four of them had been involved in the break-in.

Below: When Arthur Miller was put on trial for contempt of Congress in Washington, Marilyn accompanied him but stayed out of sight until the trial was over. When she finally did agree to speak to reporters, she told them she had spent the time reading transcripts of the proceedings in court.

Opposite: Marilyn with society hostess Elsa Maxwell at an April in Paris Ball, held in 1957.

A visit from the stork?

Above: In April 1957, Marilyn had found out she was expecting a baby. Her doctor had warned her that it might be an ectopic pregnancy, in which the fetus develops inside a fallopian tube instead of in the uterus, but she had put such thoughts out of her head and was euphoric at the thought of finally becoming a mother.

Opposite above: Onlookers laugh as Marilyn lights a super firecracker to start inaugual ceremonies at the reactivated Rockefeller Center Sidewalk Superintendents Club in New York. The firecracker triggered a dynamite blast in the excavation pit of the new 47-story Time & Life building nearby.

Opposite below: Marilyn and her husband refuse to be drawn on whether she is pregnant, as they arrive back in New York after a short vacation in Jamaica.

Although she was depressed when the pregnancy did turn out to be ectopic and had to be terminated, Marilyn still managed to put on a brave and happy face for newsmen as she left Doctors Hospital in New York with Arthur Miller in August 1957.

Conversation Piece...

Opposite: Actress Joan Copeland was Arthur Miller's sister, and when she opened in Noel Coward's *Conversation Piece*, Marilyn went to the first night party in the Barbizon Plaza Hotel to congratulate her sister-in-law.

Above and right: At the 1958 March of Dimes Fashion Show, Marilyn appeared as one of the models and was pictured with twins Lindy and Sandy Sue Solomon, who were featured on the March of Dimes poster. The charity helped children with polio, and one of the twins walked with crutches after recovering from the illness. The fashion show was held at the Waldorf-Astoria and it featured designs by members of the couture group of the New York Dress Institute, as well as other designers from New York, California and Italy. Marilyn wore a champagne-colored silk dress with a fitted jacket designed by John Moore for Talmack.

Signing up...

Above: Harold Mirisch, president of the Mirisch Company, talks to Marilyn about their upcoming production, *Some Like It Hot*, Billy Wilder and I.A.L. Diamond's screenplay based on a German movie entitled *Fanfares of Love*. Marilyn's role was supposed to be peripheral to the main action, but the minute she arrives on screen she seems to take over the movie. Despite her misgivings about playing another dumb blonde, she needed a hit when *The Prince and the Showgirl* did not do as well as expected.

Opposite and following pages: When Arthur Miller was inducted as a member of the National Institute of Arts and Letters on 21 May, 1958, Marilyn happily signed autographs for her fans.

Some Like It Hot

Opposite: Marilyn and Arthur Miller leaving New York for Hollywood, where Marilyn was to start work on *Some Like It Hot*.

Above: Co-star Tony Curtis had to spend almost the entire movie in drag, since the plot involved two male musicians who witness the Valentine's Day Massacre in 1920s New York and disguise themselves as women to escape the Mob. Curtis was uncomfortable in costume at first, but with the help of drag artist Barbette, quickly learned how to walk like a woman. Lemmon was not so adept a pupil.

Right: Director Billy Wilder discusses a scene with Marilyn. She had been dismayed to discover the picture was being shot in black and white, rather than Technicolor, as per her contract with Fox. Wilder explained that tests had shown that the thick makeup Tony Curtis and Jack Lemmon had to wear in their guise as women turned greenish when filmed in color, making them look like clowns.

Right: Joe E. Brown, who played millionaire Osgood Fielding III, chats with Marilyn on set. Fielding falls in love with "Daphne" - Jack Lemmon in drag.

Above and opposite: Marilyn as Sugar, the ukelele player in the "all-girl" band. Wilder had considered several actors for the male leads in *Some Like It Hot*, including Frank Sinatra and at an early stage Danny Kaye and Bob Hope, before settling on Curtis and then Lemmon. Despite difficulties on *The Seven Year Itch*, Wilder rated Marilyn's performance highly and cast her in the role of Sugar considering it the weakest role and therefore vital to chose the right actress for the part. Filming began in early September 1958 but Wilder and Diamond continued to work on the script during shooting.

A real artist...

Above: Marilyn shares a joke on the set of *Some Like It Hot.*

Opposite: Director Billy Wilder gives Marilyn some quiet advice. When Joe Hyams of *The New York Herald* interviewed Wilder towards the end of filming, he complained of Marilyn's unpunctuality and inability to remember lines. When asked if he would work with her again, he replied, "I have discussed this with my doctor and my psychiatrist and they tell me I'm too old and too rich to go through this again." However, this was the reaction of the moment and he later said of Marilyn, "Anyone can remember lines, but it takes a real artist to come on the set and not know her lines and yet give the performance she did!"

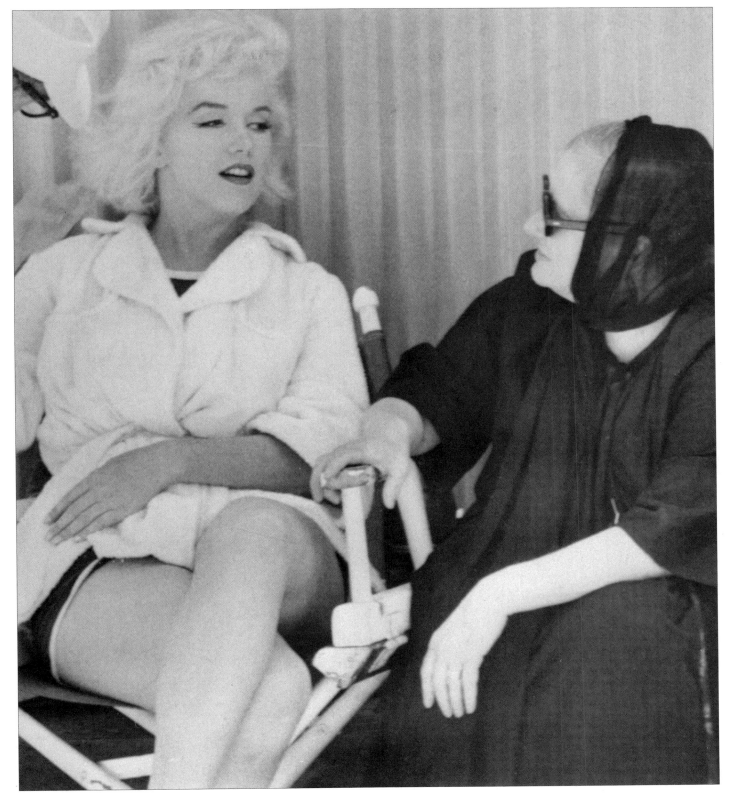

On the beach

Opposite: Tony Curtis posing as bogus oil baron Mr Shell to attract Sugar's attention. Although set in Florida, the exterior scenes were filmed at the Hotel del Coronado, a Victorian mansion built in the 1880s near San Diego which had been a haunt of the rich and famous over the years and was said to have been where Edward VIII met Mrs Simpson.

Above: Marilyn on location with Paula Strasberg. Most of Marilyn's directors had been angered by Paula's interference on set, but Wilder firmly established who was boss early on.

Marilyn pregnant

Opposite below and left: During the shooting of the bathing scene, Marilyn wore a 1920s bathing suit that was considerably more modest than most of the swimming costumes she had been photographed in previously. On the first attempt at shooting this scene, a shark was believed to have been spotted in the water, so filming had to be stopped three hours earlier than planned.

Opposite above: Marilyn chats to Arthur Miller between takes. Although he was tied up with writing commitments in New York, Miller came to Hollywood to support Marilyn as often as he could. As filming proceeded Marilyn realized she was pregnant again, and in some of her later scenes her costumes had to be let out. Unfortunately by this time she was so hooked on sleeping pills and alcohol that she was unable to give them up. Between takes she asked her assistant to bring a flask of coffee which was said to contain vermouth. By late October Marilyn had missed nearly two weeks of filming because of illness and many more hours by arriving late on set, costing the production some $200,000.

A box-office success

Above: Sugar chats to Josephine, while she takes her bath. Tony Curtis became terribly frustrated at Marilyn's inability to remember her lines, which often led to dozens of takes of simple scenes, and at her habitual lateness. At times Marilyn seemed unable to cope with even the simplest dialogues needing more than 40 takes to say "It's me, Sugar". Curtis famously commented to journalists that kissing Marilyn was "like kissing Hitler", but he later said that it was a throwaway line that had been taken far too seriously. Although Marilyn was upset she always refused to fight her battles in the Press, and merely replied that Curtis had only said it because she wore prettier dresses in the movie.

Despite all the problems during production, and even a disastrous preview, *Some Like It Hot* was a huge success at the box office, becoming one of the three top-earning pictures of 1959. It has become a classic movie, still entertaining audiences 40 years later and is counted amongst Marilyn's best-ever performances.

Opposite: Frenchman Maurice Chevalier admires Marilyn's assets as he tours the set of *Some Like It Hot*. Marilyn's rather revealing dress had been designed by Orry-Kelly who created it specifically for the picture. The movie received six Oscar nominations, including Jack Lemmon for Best Actor and Wilder for Best Director but Orry-Kelly, nominated for Best Costume Design, was the only winner.

Running wild

Opposite: A candid shot of Marilyn, taken on the beach. Her hair had been lightened to almost white for *Some Like It Hot* and it was beginning to show the strain of all those years of bleaching.

Left: Carson McCullers greets Marilyn with a kiss. The two women had known each other since Marilyn's early days in New York in 1955 when she and Marilyn had both been occupants of the Gladstone Hotel on East 52nd Street.

Above: Marilyn meets Danish author Isak Dinesen - otherwise known as Baroness Karen Blixen, author of *Out of Africa* - at the New York home of U.S. writer Carson McCullers. Both she and Arthur Miller had been invited to the event, which took place during Blixen's lecture tour of America in February 1959.

In the public eye...

Above: Arthur Miller and Marilyn attending the première of *Some Like It Hot* at Loew's Capitol Theater on Broadway in New York, on 29 March, 1959. Marilyn had lost her baby early the previous December, and had been staying out of the public eye as she recuperated.

Opposite: A Twentieth Century-Fox publicity shot, taken by Frank Powolny. Another shot in this series became the most famous picture in the world of Marilyn, when artist Andy Warhol used it as the basis for his series of silkscreen prints of her.

Opposite: Marilyn braves icy winds at La Guardia Airport as she arrives in Chicago for the release there of *Some Like It Hot*.

Above: Arthur Miller escorts Marilyn away from Lennox Hill Hospital, where she had been having corrective surgery to try to cure her chronic endometriosis. Despite appearances, their marriage was already in deep trouble as Marilyn had become convinced that her failure to give him a child would drive him away.

Exits and entrances

Opposite: Despite her feelings, as usual Marilyn put on a good show for reporters.

Left: Marilyn had always been interested in Russia - all her drama coaches had based their teaching on the work of the Russian actor and director Konstantin Stanislavsky. When the Soviet Premier Nikita krushchev visited the Fox studios during his tour of America, she flew from New York to attend the lunch in his honor and for once in her life arrived early.

Below: Arthur Miller and Marilyn arrive in New York in November 1959. She was due to begin work within a few days on *The Billionaire*, later called *Let's Make Love*, but in the event did not start on the project until early in 1960. The leading man was to have been Gregory Peck, but by the start of filming he had moved to another project and there were many problems in finding an actor to replace him. Miller had spent months working on revisions to his own screenplay for *The Misfits* and hoped that Marilyn would be free to begin shooting the movie in April 1960.

Right: Marilyn strikes a pensive pose as she listens to Nikita Krushchev speak.

Opposite: Despite looking luminously beautiful in this publicity picture, by the end of 1959, Marilyn was in a poor state of health, and the start of filming on *Let's Make Love* was delayed as she regularly called in sick. This was not unusual on occasion, but now there were days on end when she did not arrive for work. Apart from her problems with drugs and alcohol, this was also her way of showing that she was not happy with the script, and Arthur Miller was called in to rewrite whole sections of it. His involvement was never credited, as the forthcoming *The Misfits* was to be billed as both his screenwriting debut and the first time he had written anything specifically for Marilyn.

CHAPTER SIX

The Misfits

The plot of *Let's Make Love* is a comedy of mistaken identity and misunderstanding. It involves a show in production in Greenwich Village that is a satirical life history of fictional billionaire Jean-Marc Clément. The billionaire himself hears about the production, turns up at rehearsal, and falls for blonde bombshell Amanda Dell. The director mistakes him for a lookalike come to audition for the part of Jean-Marc Clément in the show - and because of his amazing resemblance he gets the part … Originally, much of the comedy depended on the fact that Jean-Marc Clément was not able to sing or dance, but was required to do so to appear in the show and get the girl - which was why Gregory Peck had originally been cast. After he dropped out, several other stars turned the part down but Miller suggested Yves Montand, who was in America touring with his one-man show. His English was poor and he was a renowned song-and-dance man, which made rather a nonsense of the plot. These drawbacks were instantly overlooked when he agreed to do the movie, because Fox were desperate to get it underway before they lost any more time. Marilyn, Miller, Montand and his wife, Simone Signoret, soon became great friends, sharing adjacent bungalows at the Beverly Hills Hotel. Marilyn went shopping with Simone, Miller coached Montand with his English. That didn't stop Montand and Marilyn starting a passionate affair after Miller left for New York to work on the script of *The Misfits*, and Signoret returned to France.

For Marilyn, the affair was not so much about falling in love as seeking attention and some much-needed affection. Miller had abandoned her again to work on his script, and although *The Misfits* was supposed to be for her, she now firmly believed it was really all about getting his own career back on track. Perhaps Marilyn also began her affair because she wanted to see how Miller would react - would he still care, would he be angry and upset and come running? The answer was no. Grateful that at last Marilyn seemed happy to be working, he decided to leave well alone. As for Montand, he was a stranger in Hollywood and was enticed into an affair with a beautiful woman, far from home. He didn't expect it to lead anywhere - and for that matter neither did Marilyn. Signoret also ignored what was going on - when asked about it later she replied that if Marilyn was in love with her husband it just proved what good taste she had.

Apart from this, the filming of *Let's Make Love* proceeded predictably, with the usual lateness on set, forgotten lines and missed calls. The major difference from Cukor's point of view was that he did not have to deal with Paula Strasberg, Marilyn having temporarily fallen out with her.

Meanwhile, Miller had virtually completed the script of *The Misfits*, which was due to begin filming in July. From the beginning he had an ambiguous and unresolved attitude to the whole project. On the one hand, he was creating a vehicle for Marilyn, and his personal life with her meant that there were themes he could not bring himself to explore. On the other, he was continually striving to repeat the success of *Death of a Salesman*, and hoped that *The Misfits* would prove to be as good, if not better. A further complication was that he took a stance of moral superiority over Hollywood - referring to Marilyn's loyal audience as "the great unwashed" - even while he was trying to tap into the success and riches of the movie business himself. He had partly resolved this to himself by hoping that *The Misfits* would not go on general release, but would be roadshowed in select movie theaters, with exclusive and expensive showings. Director John Huston quickly disabused him of this idea - it was apparent to him that what Miller had created was a potentially good and workable movie, but not a masterpiece.

Because *Let's Make Love* had run so late - not solely due to Marilyn but also because of an actors' strike - she had to go almost straight from one project to the other. Given the emotional demands that working made on her, this was always going to be dangerous because she had no time to build up her reserves again. The other problem was the nature of the material. Marilyn had hoped and believed that Miller would create an exciting and different dramatic role for her to play, but instead all he had come up with was just another version of Marilyn. He gave his character, Roslyn, feelings that Marilyn had, put words into her mouth that Marilyn had spoken, made her act just like Marilyn. When he had started he had been in love with Marilyn, so his Roslyn was in many ways an idealized and sanitized version of her. Now the Millers were almost on the point of divorce, held together only by the project, and he had a very different view of his wife. Unfortunately, he had been unable to translate this effectively into the role, so Roslyn was not a rounded person. Marilyn was devastated that he had chosen to portray her as so vulnerable, wounded and helpless, with no depth or complexity and so little to offer. It made her uncomfortable that he both refused to acknowledge her dark side, and that he had revealed so many private moments of her life on screen for all to see.

There were even more tensions and fights than usual during filming - all exacerbated by the fact they were working in the Nevada desert in July, with daytime temperatures often over 100ºF. Halfway through filming,

Marilyn's health completely broke down, and she left Nevada for Los Angeles, where she checked into the Westside Hospital for ten days. However, she returned to complete the picture, which finished shooting a month later. Not long afterwards, Marilyn and Miller announced that they had separated, and a couple of days later, her co-star Clark Gable died of a heart attack. The movie has become so famous for these events, and for the problems on set, that its quality is often overlooked. Gable gave one of his finest performances, and despite everything Marilyn is superb.

The forthcoming divorce from Miller meant yet another failure for Marilyn, who was still recovering from doing the two movies back-to-back and trying to function despite her increasing dependence on drugs. She went back to New York, hoping to find sanctuary with the Strasbergs, but instead of allowing her to rest, Strasberg talked her into agreeing to appear in Somerset Maugham's *Rain*, which he planned to direct. He felt that completing a serious acting role successfully would restore her self-esteem, but he also had no previous film credits, so he needed Marilyn to get the project off the ground.

On Christmas Eve 1960, Marilyn was alone, but suddenly a mass of flowers was delivered. The card with them said, "Best, Joe." As Marilyn said to her assistant, there was only one Joe, and from that moment he began to feature once again in her life.

Marilyn traveled to Mexico to file for divorce on 20 January, 1961, in the hopes that the inauguration of President John F. Kennedy on the same day would keep the Press occupied. A few days later she attended the preview of *The Misfits*, but she and Miller carefully avoided each other. She became even more deeply depressed afterwards, and on the advice of her analyst, Dr Kris, she signed herself into the Payne-Whitney Clinic under the name Faye Miller. In the state she was in, Marilyn probably did not realize that the Payne-Whitney was a psychiatric hospital. She had always been terrified of going mad and being locked away, because she believed her family had a

Previous page: Marilyn strikes a pose during a number for *Let's Make Love*, which went into production at the beginning of 1960. This time the biggest delay to filming was not caused by either Marilyn's lateness or ill health but a strike by actors to preserve residual payments, later joined by The Writers' Guild, shut down production for several months.

Opposite: Marilyn and Yves Montand rehearse on set. At a cocktail party to welcome Montand to Hollywood, Marilyn told reporters that next to her husband and Marlon Brando, Montand was the most attractive man she knew. What she did not mention was that she had told friends in private that he reminded her of Joe DiMaggio.

history of insanity. Her great-grandfather
had committed suicide, her grandfather
had died in hospital suffering from
dementia, and her grandmother, Della, had
been diagnosed as a manic-depressive. In
addition, her mother, Gladys, had spent
years going in and out of various hospitals.
However, the facts may not be quite so
straightforward. Her great-grandfather had
killed himself when his health was failing
and his farm was about to be repossessed -
and many people committed suicide during
the Great Depression of the 1930s. Her
grandfather had suffered dementia, but
later study of his medical records seemed to
show it was almost certainly caused by an
infection that attacked his brain tissue - and
not by an inherited weakness. Her
grandmother, Della, died of heart disease
and had also suffered a stroke, both of
which can lead to erratic behavior, and
there is no real evidence that she was
psychotic. As for Gladys, she certainly
suffered from depression, but at the time
the illness was often not properly
diagnosed, while the effects of new drugs
were not fully understood. Several of her
friends believed that a temporary inability
to cope became a lifelong incapacity, purely
because of the effect of the drugs she was
prescribed.

However, when Marilyn realized
where she was, she apparently broke a glass
door with a chair and threatened to cut
herself if she was not immediately released.
Attendants subdued her, and carried her to

Right: Marilyn rehearsing a dance number in
Let's Make Love.

Opposite: Clark Gable and Marilyn in a scene
from *The Misfits,* which was filmed during the
summer of 1960 in Nevada. Gable resembled
the picture of the man that Gladys had told
the young Norma Jeane was her father, and
when she was a child Marilyn had often
fantasized that she really was the daughter of
the famous movie star.

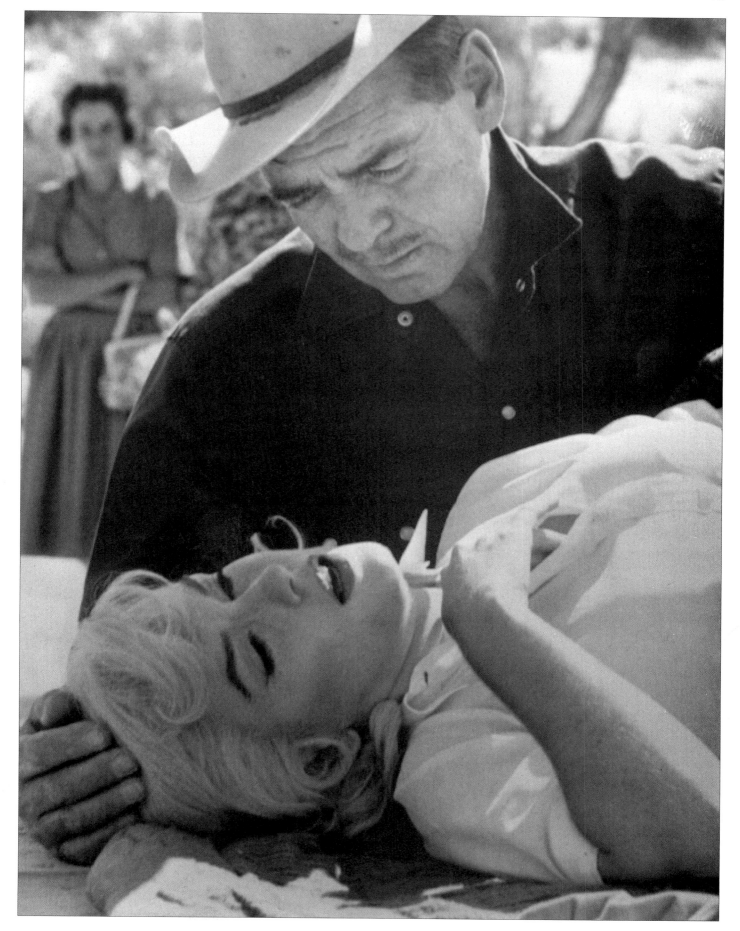

the ward for violent patients, where she was sedated and restrained. She tried to contact the Strasbergs, but it was DiMaggio who finally found her and obtained her release. Although doctors initially said she was not fit to leave, he insisted that she was transferred and took her to the Columbia-Presbyterian Medical Center - another hospital, but at least not a psychiatric one.

Despite all this, Strasberg was still trying to get *Rain* off the ground, and Fox were pushing her to make a comedy called *Goodbye, Charlie* as the last picture they were owed under her contract. No one seemed to realize that it was largely the way she worked that had put her in hospital in the first place. In the event, Cukor, the approved director for *Goodbye, Charlie*, dropped out of the project and none of the other directors named in her contract could do it - except Lee Strasberg. He suddenly ceased to object to Marilyn making another comedy when he saw the chance to command a fee as her director. In the event, the fee he wanted was too large, and Fox agreed to forgo the project as long as Marilyn agreed that they were still owed a movie. Strasberg's own project, *Rain*, also fell through and Marilyn refused to make it without him.

After Marilyn had left the hospital, DiMaggio had taken her off to Florida, where he was working with the Yankees during their spring training. There she sat in the sun, walked on the beach and generally enjoyed DiMaggio's company - although they were now just friends and there was no possibility of a new marriage. It was not the end of her health problems - she was admitted to hospital twice more that year: for an operation to correct an unspecified internal problem, and for surgery to remove her gall bladder.

Back in Hollywood in the summer of 1961, Marilyn was soon involved in the world of endless parties and entertaining, and it was inevitable that she would be invited to Peter Lawford's beach house. She already knew Lawford from her early days in Hollywood, and he was a friend of Sinatra, but Lawford's parties were now the ones to be invited to because he was married to Pat Kennedy. Sooner or later his brothers-in-law, the President and the Attorney-General, would be attending. It was at Lawford's house that Marilyn met both Kennedy brothers, and although she may have had a fling with the President, it was Bobby Kennedy with whom she started a more serious affair.

The dream of a new life in New York was now well and truly over, so Marilyn decided to base herself back in Hollywood, although she still kept her Manhattan apartment. She found a small apartment on Doheny Drive, in the same house in which she had lived when she first became a star nearly seven years earlier. It may have seemed like coming home, but perhaps it was just an attempt to pretend that the last few years had not happened.

Left: Marilyn prepares to film a dance scene from *Let's Make Love*. It was a rehearsal within a rehearsal, as the movie was set backstage as a theater company puts together a satirical play with song and dance routines. She performed several of her routines with famed song-and-dance man Frankie Vaughan.

Welcome to Hollywood!

On 15 January, 1960, Twentieth Century-Fox hosted a cocktail party in Hollywood to welcome Yves Montand - who was to co-star in *Let's Make Love* with Marilyn. He was not the first choice - Gregory Peck had originally been slated for the part, but had to drop out after delays in filming meant the dates would clash with other commitments. Several other well-known actors, including Cary Grant and Jimmy Stewart, had turned the part down, before Arthur Miller suggested Montand. At the time, Miller was working on rewrites of the script of *Let's Make Love* and was desperate to finish the movie so Marilyn could move on to his project, *The Misfits*.

Above: Marilyn flanked by co-stars Frankie Vaughan and Yves Montand at the cocktail party. Part of the reason for the party was also to introduce the cast to the Press. Montand was not well known in America - and his English was far from fluent - but his recent one-man shows in Los Angeles and New York had been a great success.

Left and opposite: Right from the start there was a certain chemistry between Marilyn and Montand - and it was not long before they started a passionate love affair.

Let's Make Love...

Arthur Miller and Yves Montand became great friends even before filming started - Montand had appeared in the French production of Miller's play, *The Crucible*. Montand's wife, Simone Signoret, and Marilyn also got on very well. At the start of filming *Let's Make Love* the two couples rented adjacent bungalows at the Beverly Hills Hotel and spent a great deal of time together. However, in April 1960 Miller returned to New York, leaving Marilyn to finish work on the movie, while Simone Signoret had already returned to France. It was almost inevitable that Marilyn and Montand, left alone together, would begin a relationship.

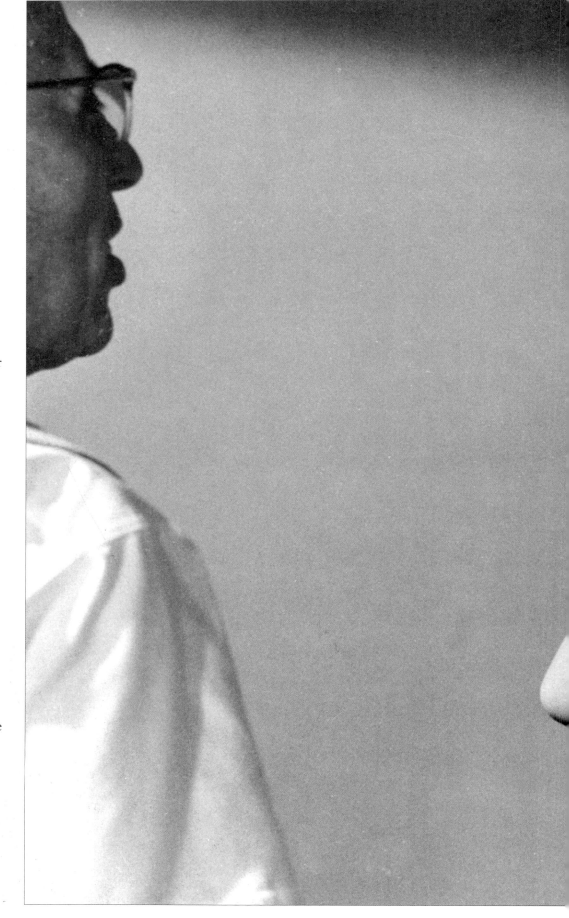

Right: Director George Cukor discusses a scene with Marilyn. Choreographer Jack Cole had worked out the dance sequences for *Let's Make Love.* Cole had worked on all Marilyn's dance routines since *Gentlemen Prefer Blondes* in 1953. She trusted him implicitly and had specifically requested his services for *Let's Make Love.* Cukor, exasperated at having to deal with Marilyn's constant lateness and insecurities, left much of the direction of the dance scenes to Cole. Marilyn and Cole were firm personal friends, but working on this project strained their relationship to the limit. Marilyn's marriage to Arthur Miller was unraveling fast, and her intake of pills was rising rapidly. Studio executives were also alarmed that she didn't look as good on camera as usual - the daily rushes were often disappointing. Despite all her problems, she had always managed to produce something magical for the camera - but this time it was not to be.

Too many curves?

At the start of filming Marilyn was quite svelte, but during the enforced halt caused by the actors' and writers' strike during March 1960 she put on a considerable amount of weight and in some later scenes - like the one opposite - she looks distinctly chubby. Cukor complained that this meant it took much longer to set up each scene as he had to film Marilyn from the most flattering angle.

My Heart Belongs to Daddy...

Right: Studio head Buddy Adler complained that Marilyn looked so overweight in the first version of this dance sequence that it seemed as if she was pregnant. He also hated the chalky-white makeup that had been developed for her role, similar to that used in *Bus Stop*. In *Bus Stop* it had been appropriate, as her character of Cherie worked nights and slept through the day, but now it made her look even more unhealthy. Producer Jerry Wald tried to assure him that the dance sequence would be so fast-paced in the final edit that the audience would not notice Marilyn's looks.

However, delays in filming had caused the movie to be $500,000 over budget, and despite all their concerns about Marilyn's appearance, there were to be no retakes.

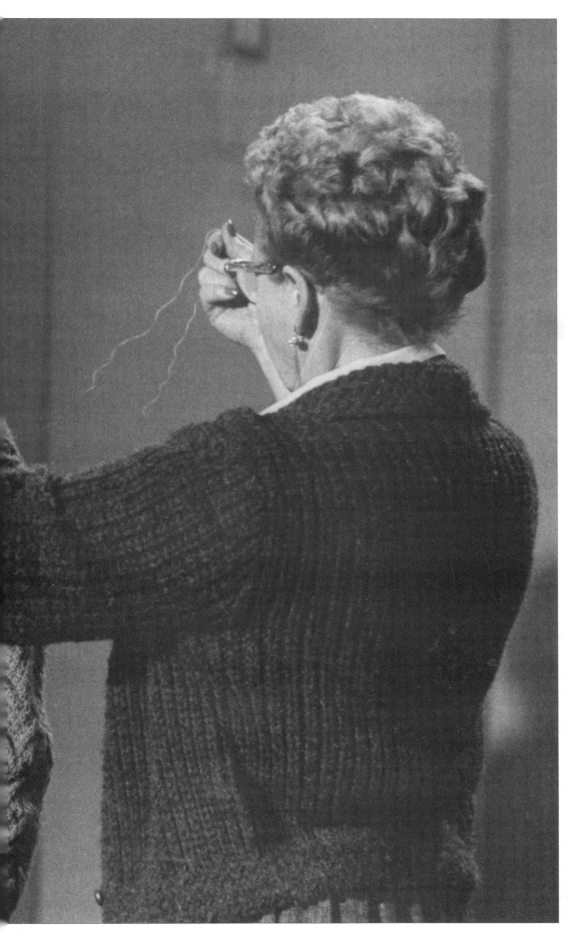

Sewn in...

Left: Adler also explained that a major reason for the "bumpy" look round Marilyn's middle was that the sweater she was wearing had been sewn to her leotard, causing it to move strangely and ride up. He claimed that if the stitching was removed, the sweater would move loosely and naturally and the problem would be solved. Marilyn had been working on set on her own, filming all the song and dance sequences, and she had yet to complete the bulk of her scenes with Montand, even though the proposed start date for *The Misfits* was now looming.

Take it from the top...

Left: Marilyn in pensive mood on the set of *Let's Make Love.*

Below: A still from the finished scene, in which Marilyn dances and sings Cole Porter's "My Heart Belongs to Daddy".

Opposite: However bad she was feeling, Marilyn could always raise a smile for the camera. Since early January 1960, she had been seeing a new psychoanalyst, Dr Ralph Greenson, who had been recommended by her analyst in New York. Greenson tried to limit her intake of pills and to help her regain some kind of composure so she could complete the movie. He was to remain her analyst until her death, some two years later.

Celebration!

Opposite: Twentieth Century Fox studio head Buddy Adler welcomes Marilyn as she arrives to complete *Let's Make Love.*

Left: Marilyn proudly displays her Golden Globe award, which had just been presented by members of the Hollywood Foreign Press Association for her performance as the "Best Actress in a Motion Picture Comedy" in *Some Like It Hot.* Many were surprised that she had not also been nominated for a "Best Actress" award at that year's Oscars but Marilyn warmly congratulated Simone Signoret, who had been nominated for her role in *Room at the Top.*

Below: At a party on set, Marilyn celebrates her birthday with the cast and crew of *Let's Make Love* where they gave her a seed pearl necklace. Filming was finished by mid June with only dubbing to complete but even this was subject to endless delays when Marilyn put off returning to work until mid July.

Off to Reno...

Left: Gail Sawyer, daughter of Nevada Governor Grant Sawyer, presents Marilyn with a bouquet of roses as she arrives at Reno Airport to begin work on *The Misfits*. Miller had embarked on writing the script for Marilyn as a way of showing his love for her, but as the relationship disintegrated she viewed it less as a gift of love and more as him using her name to get his first screenplay off the ground.

Opposite: Marilyn poses for photographers with her usual carefree smile intact - despite the fact that Montand had now returned to France and his wife, so her very public affair with him was over.

Below: A scene from *The Misfits*, in which Gay (Clark Gable) and Roslyn (Marilyn) plant lettuces in the garden.

The Misfits

Right: Marilyn poses with some of the cast and crew of *The Misfits.* At the top of the picture is Arthur Miller, with Eli Wallach below him, and at the front are Montgomery Clift, Marilyn and Clark Gable. Director John Huston is standing behind Marilyn.

Below: Arthur Miller and Clark Gable chat on set. The part of Gay Langland had first been offered to Robert Mitchum, but he found the script "incomprehensible".

Opposite: Marilyn played Roslyn Tabor, in Reno to get a divorce from her husband. She drives a seriously dented automobile, as men are always driving into her to get an introduction. Marilyn felt the character of Roslyn was too sweet and saccharine to be at all believable.

Director John Huston, Marilyn and Arthur Miller confer on set. All the way through shooting Miller was rewriting and adjusting the script and was still unable to decide how the piece would end. Although Huston had at first said it was "magnificent", he still felt it needed serious cuts and revisions. Miller hoped he had written a great American story, something to rival his most successful play, *Death of a Salesman*, but Huston was more realistic and could see that the story was deeply flawed. Miller believed in his creation so much that he was unable to step back and reappraise it. Marilyn was hurt and angry that Roslyn, who was so obviously based on herself, revealed no elements of her own dark side. She felt this was due to Miller's inability to accept this aspect of her life - and took it as a rejection of the person she really was.

Don't shoot!

Above: Roslyn begs Gay not to shoot the rabbits that have eaten their newly-planted lettuces. Marilyn herself was very sentimental about wild animals and hated to see them hurt.

Opposite: Gable gives Marilyn a big hug. Despite the heat and the strain of waiting for Marilyn, he did not turn against her. When he died of a heart attack soon after shooting finished, many people blamed her behavior for causing him stress, but it was more likely his insistence on doing some of his own stunts or the fact that he was a heavy smoker that had led to the problems with his heart. On set Gable was calm and patient with both Marilyn and Montgomery Clift who was also a troubled personality. However, Marilyn said of Clift that she was "the only person I know who's in worse shape than me".

Following pages: A close-up of Marilyn, in one of the many wigs made for her to wear in the movie, and Gable.

A not so happy couple...

Opposite and above: Arthur Miller and Marilyn on the set of *The Misfits* in 1960, as filming is coming to an end. Although they still kept up the pretense of being together in public, it is noticeable that in these pictures Marilyn does not have her usual bright smile or sparkle, and that there seems to be a certain distance between husband and wife. By the time shooting was nearly over there were rumors that Miller was having an affair with Inge Morath, a young photographer who was visiting the set and Marilyn had moved into Paula Strasberg's suite at the hotel. Only a week after the film wrapped they announced their plans to divorce.

Strange bedfellows?

Left: Strangely prescient of a relationship which was to develop between Marilyn and John and Robert Kennedy, a theater-owner in Spokane, Washington, advertises a speech by presidential nominee Senator John F. Kennedy, next to Marilyn's name - one of her movies is currently showing inside.

Above: During filming of *The Misfits* the cast and crew were often working out in the boiling sun in the desert, and Marilyn was careful to shade her skin.

Opposite: With no Montand and Miller on his way out, Marilyn was ready to give love a miss for a while and concentrate on sorting out her life instead. While making *The Misfits* her health had deteriorated to such a state that she had to be hospitalized for several days. Her dependence on prescription drugs had made it almost impossible for her to work and by the time filming was over Marilyn was at a very low ebb.

Putting on a happy face...

Left: Montgomery Clift and Marilyn arrive at Capitol Theater on Broadway on 31 January 1961, for a preview of *The Misfits*. Miller was also there with his children, but the two of them avoided each other. A typical review from the *New York Daily News* said, "Miss Monroe has seldom looked worse; the camera is unfailingly unflattering. But there is a delicacy about her playing and a tenderness that is affecting."

Below and opposite: Marilyn leaves the Columbia-Presbyterian Medical Center, where she had spent three weeks trying to pull herself out of the depths of depression.

In and out of hospital...

Above: Joe DiMaggio, who was in Florida helping to coach the New York Yankees during their spring training session, invited Marilyn to join him there to recuperate after her release from the Columbia-Presbyterian Hospital. In Florida she spent long periods in the sun relaxing and renewing her friendship with Joe.

Opposite top: Joe arrives to visit Marilyn in the Polyclinic Hospital in New York in June 1961, where she had undergone an operation to have her gall bladder removed. It was the fifth time she had been admitted to hospital in ten months.

Opposite bottom: A frail-looking Marilyn is discharged from hospital nearly two weeks later. As usual, the Press were there in force.

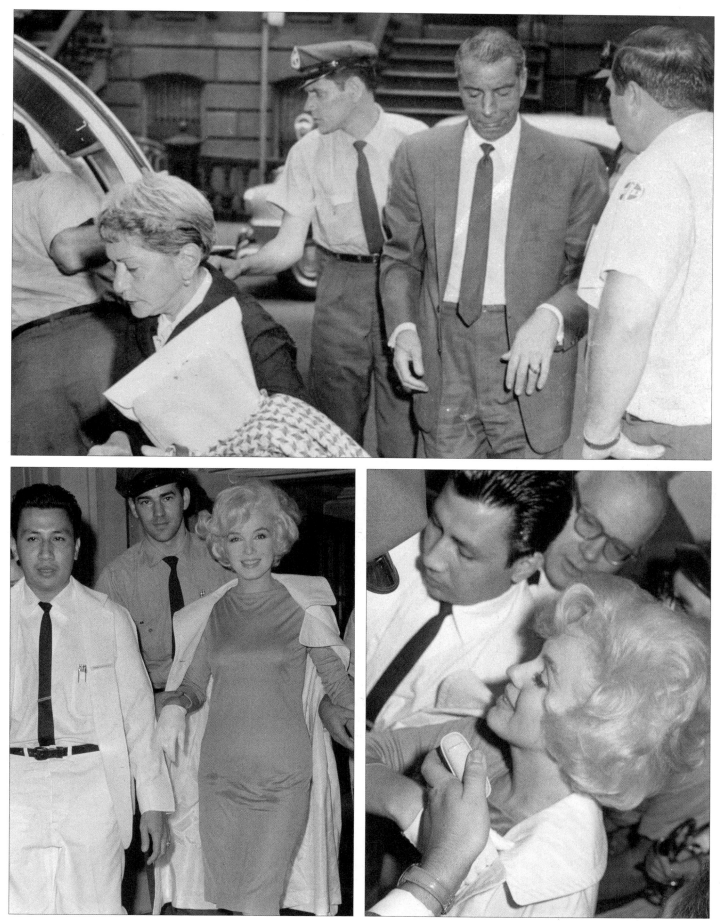

CHAPTER SEVEN

Something's Got To Give

At the beginning of 1962, Marilyn was seeing her analyst, Dr Ralph Greenson, every day. There are mixed views about his treatment of Marilyn. On the one hand, he was undoubtedly totally committed to her, but on the other, many believe that he became far too emotionally involved and had lost any semblance of objective distance. Even more controversially, he involved Marilyn in his home life - as he did to an extent with some other patients - and she often had dinner there after her sessions, sometimes stayed overnight and had even spent her last Christmas with his family. One of the first rules of psychoanalysis is that the analyst should avoid personal involvement, but Greenson appeared to believe that traditional methods had failed with Marilyn, and that what she actually needed was to experience a normal, stable family life. His detractors accuse him of wanting to control Marilyn - as many men had tried to do before - and he certainly attempted to screen who she saw. His friend, Eunice Murray, became her housekeeper, and it was Murray who found the house on Fifth Helena Drive that became Marilyn's last home. Marilyn liked it because it was a Mexican-style building that was reminiscent of Greenson's house.

Excited about having a proper home of her own, Marilyn planned to fly to Mexico to buy furniture, artwork and tiles so she could create the same kind of colorful Mexican décor that she had enjoyed at the Greenson house. By all accounts she hoped the move would mark yet another new beginning, and in an effort to tie up loose ends, she had agreed to do *Something's Got To Give* for Fox,

to complete her studio commitment. Unfortunately, in the midst of this positive atmosphere, word came that Miller was to marry again. The news affected Marilyn badly - it brought back all her lost dreams of being a good wife, having a family and creating a home. When she came back from Mexico, she had obviously slipped back into the old cycle of too many pills, mixed with too much champagne.

A few days after her return, Marilyn arrived at the Golden Globe Awards, obviously the worse for drink. When she collected her statuette for World's Favorite Female Star, her acceptance speech was rambling and inconclusive and gossip started in Hollywood that she was finished. Despite this, a couple of weeks later Marilyn had pulled herself together enough to report for costume fitting and makeup tests for her new movie, and the studio breathed a sigh of relief.

The plot of *Something's Got To Give* was based on *My Favorite Wife*, a popular 1940 comedy about a woman who has been shipwrecked on a desert island for many years and is believed dead, but who finally returns home to find her husband is married to another woman. The original script needed work and Marilyn was delighted when Fox appointed Nunnally Johnson to rewrite it. Johnson had written the screenplay for *How to Marry a Millionaire*, and although Marilyn had spent years trying to get away from the kind of dumb blonde character he had created, she now knew she desperately needed a big hit to boost her reputation and silence wagging tongues. Anyway, the role of Ellen Arden would be different, because for the first time she would be playing a wife and mother. Another inducement was her co-star, Dean

Martin, and Fox had also appointed Cukor to direct, with whom Marilyn had worked on *Let's Make Love*.

Johnson created a script that Marilyn was pleased with, and which incorporated many of her ideas, but he left the project before filming began. A series of other scriptwriters then worked on it and Marilyn became increasingly unhappy as the screenplay moved away from Johnson's version. New pages were always sent out to cast and crew on different-colored paper, so that everyone could be sure they were working from the same sheet, but at one point the studio resorted to sending rewritten pages on white paper to Marilyn, to try to fool her that no changes were being made.

Because of the script problems, shooting was put back until 23 April, but by then Marilyn was ill and Dean Martin also failed to appear as he was still working on another movie. Although Marilyn managed several days' work over the next few weeks, she spent much more time at home with a fever - although she continued to work there with Paula Strasberg, trying to make some sense of the rewrites that continued to arrive daily. She now often went to see Greenson twice a day.

In the middle of all this, Greenson and his wife left for a long-planned trip to Europe. Greenson said later that he had become worried about Marilyn's increasing dependence on him, and that he himself desperately needed a break from the pressures of dealing with her. The week after he left, Marilyn turned up at the studio early and worked hard each day. She had been invited to sing "Happy Birthday" to the President at a gala forty-fifth birthday salute at Madison Square Garden and she was desperate to go. The previous week, there had been a great deal of publicity about the fact that Miller had been an honored guest at a presidential dinner party for the French Minister of Culture, and Marilyn was determined not to miss the chance to show that she was a presidential favorite too. Nevertheless, the studio was reluctant to let her go, because filming of *Something's Got To Give* was running so far behind.

On Thursday 17 May, Marilyn worked until noon, then flew to New York to prepare for Saturday night. She came on as the finale, singing the simple song in an outrageously sexy way that delighted the entire audience. By Sunday evening she was on her way back to Los Angeles, ready to start work again on Monday morning, and she continued to report for filming the following week. As far as

she was concerned she had only missed one day, and that was that. The studio executives at Fox saw it differently. At the time the entire movie industry was going through upheaval, and the old guard at Fox were being criticized for indulging the stars and giving in to their whims at the expense of the stockholders. In Italy *Cleopatra* was being filmed with Elizabeth Taylor and Richard Burton, and although it had already cost millions it was still going over budget; Fox had been forced to sell off part of its back lot to pay for it all. It was the wrong moment for Marilyn to challenge the studio's authority.

Behind the scenes, there was already talk of either closing the movie down or firing Marilyn and replacing her with someone else. Whether or not she was aware of these rumors, Marilyn continued to work intermittently, and relations with Cukor deteriorated. On 1 June she celebrated her thirty-sixth birthday with the cast and crew, and maybe the thought of getting older affected her badly, as it was the last day she appeared on set. The following week, desperate negotiations went on between her agent and Fox, in conjunction with Greenson - who had been hastily called back from his trip. Despite assurances that Marilyn would be back at work after a week's rest, Fox fired her from the movie. They had intended to replace her with Lee Remick, but Dean Martin refused to hear of it, saying he had signed to co-star with Marilyn and if she wasn't part of the deal, then neither was he. For the moment the picture was put on hold, while everyone considered their options.

In Marilyn's camp, they knew they needed some good publicity, and fast, to counteract the rumors that she had finally had a complete breakdown. Just before the movie closed down, Marilyn had done a photo session on set in which she swam in a pool, and had mischievously removed her costume under water. The resulting nudes were sensational, and they were quickly released - one appeared on the cover of *Life* magazine at the end of the month. Another high-profile photography session was organized with Bert Stern, for *Vogue*. The publicity and the groundswell of public opinion, which was sympathetic to Marilyn, did make Fox think again. By mid-July Marilyn was

Previous page: A publicity shot for Marilyn's ill-fated last movie, *Something's Got to Give*.

Opposite: But for the hair that has escaped from under the scarf, Marilyn almost succeeds in disguising herself as she uncharacteristically avoids the camera.

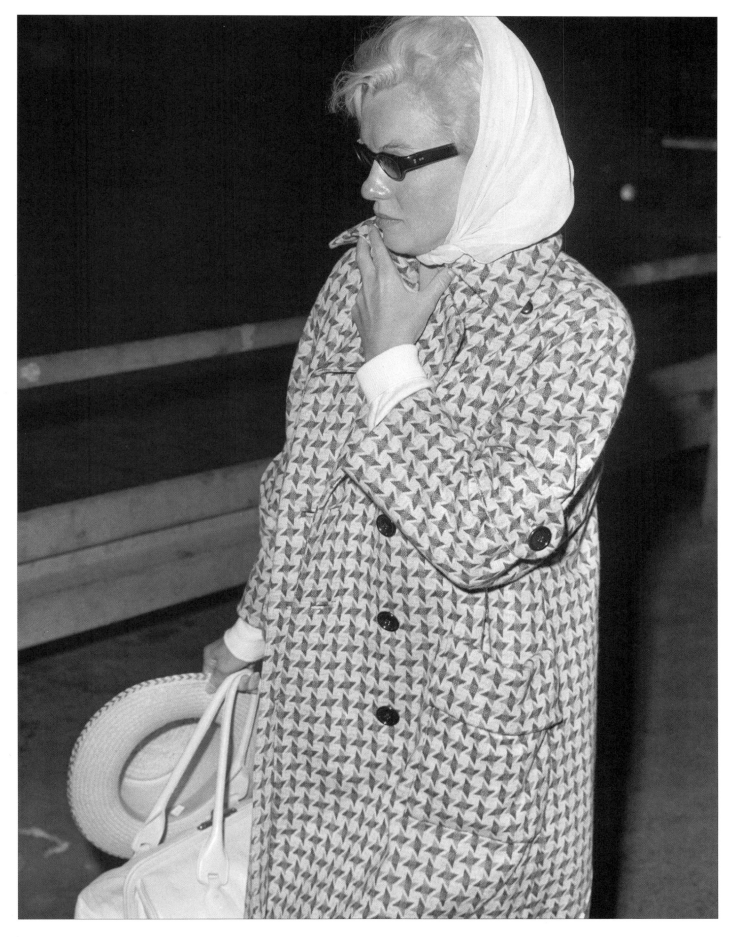

Right: Marilyn rushing out of the Yankee Clipper Hotel in Florida, after visiting the Yankee Clipper himself, Joe DiMaggio. Their marriage had been short-lived but now, as in 1954 when they were first dating, Marilyn appreciated Joe's loyalty and steadying influence.

informed that they had agreed in principle to reinstate her, although final details of the deal were still being worked out and filming could not begin again until early September because Dean Martin was fulfilling other commitments.

It seemed as if, once again, Marilyn would manage to turn disaster into triumph, but in reality those close to her were worried about whether she was currently capable of working. Unlike previous times when she had been down and apparently out, but had come back fighting, this time she seemed to be finding it more difficult.

On 3 August, Marilyn persuaded Dr Engelberg to give her a prescription for twenty-five Nembutal tablets. Engelberg and Greenson had been working together to control her drug intake, but for some reason they did not communicate about this prescription. The following day, Greenson came to Marilyn's house and spent much of the afternoon with her. She had been invited to dinner at Lawford's house, and Greenson was also going out to dinner so he left around 7.00 pm. Nearly an hour later, Lawford called to find out if Marilyn was coming over, and was concerned at her slurred speech. When Marilyn finished the call by telling him goodbye, alarm bells rang and he in turn telephoned Marilyn's lawyer, Milton Rudin, who called her housekeeper. Eunice Murray assured him that Marilyn was fine. It was not until the early hours of 5 August that Murray became concerned that the light was still on in Marilyn's room. Everyone knew she was unable to sleep if there was the slightest chink of light in the room, and her bedroom was always fitted with blackout drapes. Murray called Greenson, and the two of them broke into the room, to find Marilyn sprawled across the bed, the telephone receiver still in her hand. She had been dead for some time, and an autopsy showed large amounts of both Nembutal and chloral hydrate in her system.

The theories about Marilyn's death could - and have - filled many books, and they range from a straightforward suicide to conspiracy and murder. The reality is that no one really knows the truth. She had certainly tried to commit suicide in the past, and she had also taken accidental overdoses. Given her lifestyle, it is also possible that additional medication was obtained from someone unaware of what she had already taken. However, it is highly unlikely that she was murdered, and none of the motives so far proposed hold water under close examination. The real tragedy is that previously she had always been found in time, and this time she wasn't.

Marilyn's funeral was held at Westwood Memorial Park, in Los Angeles, and was arranged by Joe DiMaggio with the help of her half-sister, Berniece Miracle, and her business manager, Inez Melson. DiMaggio refused to allow her Hollywood friends to attend, holding them morally responsible for her death, and Press and photographers were kept at a distance. Her trusted makeup man, Whitey Snyder, did her makeup for her final appearance, fulfilling a promise made as a joke many years previously. DiMaggio also fulfilled an old promise, arranging for a single red rose to be delivered to her grave twice a week.

Even many years after her death, Marilyn Monroe is still one of the greatest legends of the twentieth century. In her movies she projected a unique and fascinating persona - a child-woman who was both innocent and full of sexuality, someone whom men desired, but who women found unthreatening. In real life, she was a beautiful and complex woman who felt deeply insecure, and who just wanted to be loved enough to wipe out her unhappy past. In her brief career she appeared in several classic movies, as well as many more that are memorable only for her presence.

It was perhaps inevitable that Marilyn Monroe the person would die young, but Marilyn Monroe the star is an extraordinary and unforgettable woman whose legend still lives on.

Flying down to Mexico...

Above: Joe gives Marilyn a goodbye kiss as she leaves for Mexico City on a short vacation in February 1962. She was traveling there to buy some Mexican-style furnishings for her newly acquired home in Hollywood. She had admired the style in the home of her analyst, Dr Ralph Greenson. Marilyn had not worked since shooting on *The Misfits* had finished towards the end of 1960, but the studio intended that she should begin filming *Something's Got to Give* as soon as rewrites to the script were complete.

Left: Marilyn waves to newsmen on her return from Mexico City in March 1962. However, she was not in good spirits having heard that Arthur Miller had remarried.

Opposite: A small white poodle, called Maf, had been given to Marilyn to keep her company after she had spent some time in a psychiatric hospital the previous year. Like many of her pets it was not properly house-trained. After she died, Maf went to live with Frank Sinatra's secretary, Gloria Lovell. Many people believe it was Sinatra who had given her the dog, but it may also have been her publicist, Pat Newcomb.

Female World Film Favorite 1961

In March 1962, Marilyn was presented with an award as Female World Film Favorite 1961 by the Foreign Press Association at their Annual Award ceremony in Hollywood.

Opposite: Actor Rock Hudson presented the award to Marilyn, and seemed almost as pleased as she was. Her slim and glamorous new look belied the fact that she was both physically and mentally fragile.

Above: Marilyn arrives for party after the ceremony with Mexican screenwriter José Bolaños. They had met during her recent trip to Mexico City, and after her death he told the world that they had planned to marry. However, the relationship didn't last for long.

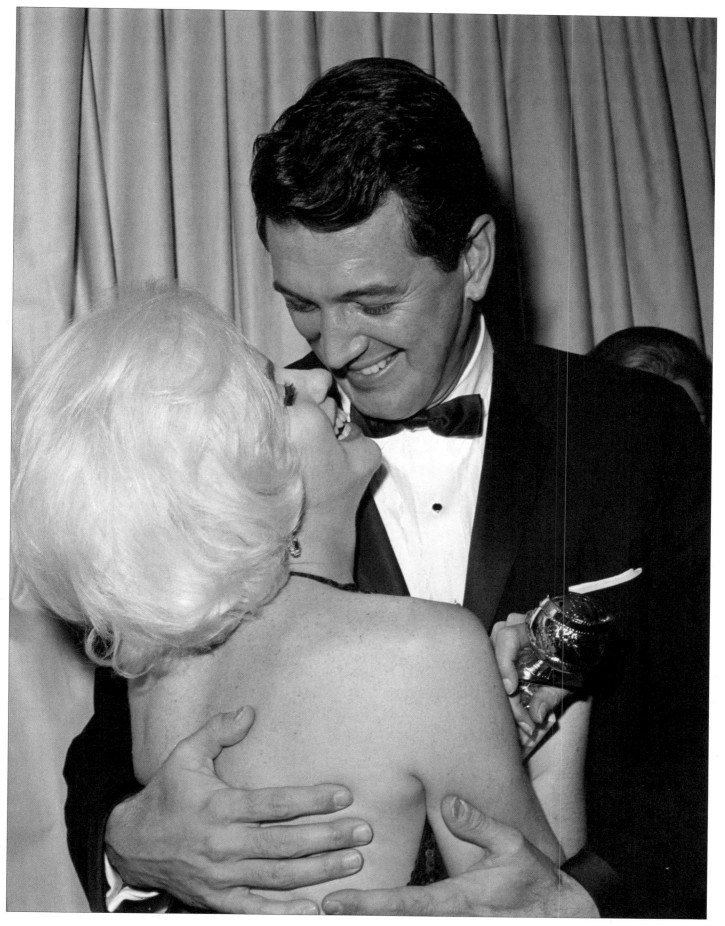

Happy Birthday, Mr President

Opposite: Marilyn sings "Happy Birthday" to President John F. Kennedy at a fund-raising event at Madison Square Garden in May 1962. She was ushered on stage by Peter Lawford, who introduced her as "the late Marilyn Monroe". After she had sung the first verse alone, she invited the audience to join in as a six-foot cake with 45 oversized candles was carried onstage.

Above: During a swimming scene in *Something's Got to Give*, when the Press had been invited on set to take some pictures, Marilyn caused a sensation by removing her swimming costume underwater. Progress on the picture had been painfully slow at a time when the studio could ill-afford to lose money and the atmosphere on set was tense. Although Marilyn looked superficially slimmer and fitter than she had done in several years, she was unable to function without medication and constant support from Dr Greenson, her psychoanalyst.

Skinny-dipping

Above: When she emerged from the pool photographers snapped nude pictures and these stunning images were immediately released for publication. One of them was used on the cover of *Life* magazine in June 1962.

Opposite: Marilyn as Eve Arden in *Something's Got to Give.* Very little of it was completed before Marilyn was fired from the picture on 8 June 1962. The following year the script was revised yet again and the movie was made as *Move Over Darling,* with Doris Day in Marilyn's role, and James Garner taking the Dean Martin part.

Right: On her 36th birthday, and on one of her last public appearances, Marilyn came onto the field at Chavez Ravine Dodger Stadium in Los Angeles, along with outfielder Albie Pearson, before a Yankees v Angels benefit game on 1 June 1962. She was appealing for donations to the Muscular Dystrophy fund.

Day of the dead...

Above: After Marilyn was found dead, on 5 August 1962, the police were called to her home on Fifth Helena Drive. They searched unsuccessfully for a suicide note, and interviewed her analyst, Dr Ralph Greenson, Dr Engelberg, and housekeeper Eunice Murray. Reporters were prevented from approaching, but photographers look pictures of Marilyn's house with the two toy stuffed dogs on the lawn.

Left: Mrs Eunice Murray, Marilyn's housekeeper and companion, leaves the house with handyman Norman Jeffries after the body has been removed to the mortuary. It was Eunice who called Dr Greenson, after apparently becoming concerned that the light was still on in Marilyn's room. When the two of them broke the door down it was too late to rouse her. Eunice had been given her job on the recommendation of Dr Greenson. She had no formal training as a nurse, but he often used her as a companion to patients of his who he felt needed day-to-day support. She did not normally stay overnight at Marilyn's house, but on the night of the star's death she had slept in one of the spare rooms.

An empty home...

Above: The bedroom where Marilyn's body was found. She had still not really settled into the house, and much of the furniture and many of the decorative pieces she had ordered in Mexico had not yet been delivered. There were piles of bags in many corners, as there was no storage. The house was in Spanish-colonial style and was L-shaped with a small guest house. Much of the interior was painted white - like most of the other places Marilyn had lived.

Left: After Marilyn's body was taken away, the police sealed all the rooms in the house. When her estate was released, the house and much of its contents was bought by Mr and Mrs Gilbert Nunez. Many of the items that had once belonged to Marilyn were auctioned off by their children in 1997.

Cause of death?

The autopsy report on Marilyn concluded that she had died of "acute barbiturate poisoning - ingestion of overdose". There were no signs of any external violence, but she had 8mg of chloral hydrate and 4.5mg of Nembutal in her bloodstream. The theories as to how this happened range from suicide, through accidental overdose to murder.

Marilyn's funeral took place at the Westwood Funeral Chapel and was arranged by her old love, Joe DiMaggio. During the service she lay in an open casket, dressed in green. Her makeup man, Whitey Snyder, had done her makeup for the very last time - having been fortified by a large amount of gin. Joe had refused to allow her Hollywood friends to attend. So there were only thirty-one invited mourners including the Strasbergs, the Greenson family and several of Marilyn's employees. Arthur Miller chose not to attend.

Opposite top: A police officer stands guard over the crypt where Marilyn will be laid to rest.

Opposite bottom: Marilyn's casket is carried out of the Westwood Park Chapel, past a line of guards.

Grief stricken

Above: Joe DiMaggio, and his son Joe DiMaggio Jr. - in his U.S. Marine dress uniform - stand shoulder to shoulder at Marilyn's funeral. Joe Jr had been one of the last people to speak to Marilyn on the phone.

Opposite above: Marilyn's psychoanalyst, Dr Ralph Greenson, with his wife and two children, at the funeral.

Opposite below: Joe is overcome by emotion as the casket is taken from the hearse and placed on a stand in front of the crypt. A recent biography of DiMaggio claims that the day of the funeral - 8 August, 1962 - was to have been the day that he and Marilyn were to remarry.

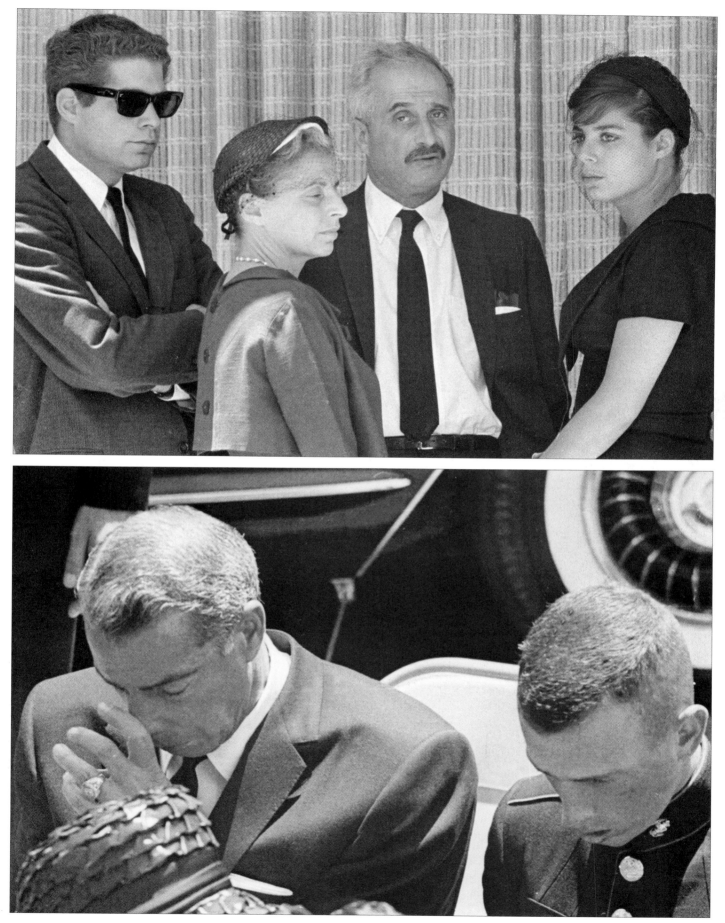

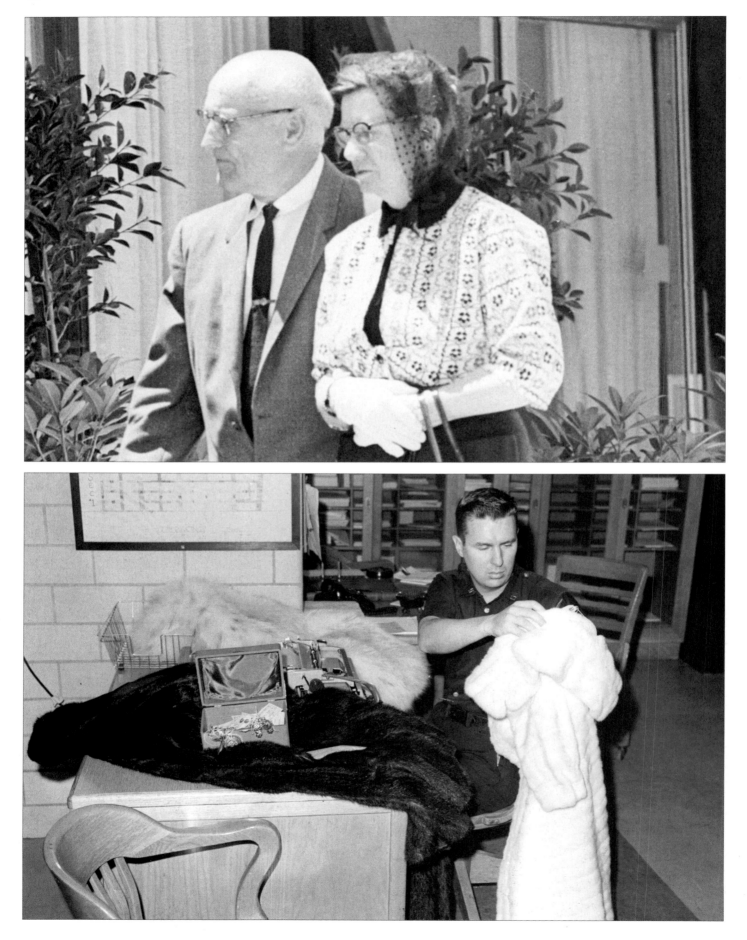

The aftermath...

Opposite top: Sam and Enid Knebelcamp were the only foster parents of Marilyn's to attend the funeral. She lived with them during the late 1930s, when Grace McKee Goddard temporarily was unable to look after her ward.

Opposite bottom: Marilyn's furs and jewelry were still in police safekeeping for some time after her death. The bulk of her estate was left to Lee Strasberg, with part of it going to Dr Kris to further the work of a psychiatric institution. Dr Kris selected the Anna Freud Foundation in London where it has been used to fund the Monroe Young Family Centre. At first most of the money went in taxes, and nothing was paid out to any of the beneficiaries for nearly ten years. Later on, her percentage of the profits from later movies began to flow through - and then royalties from merchandising and licensing. Current income is in millions of dollars.

Left: Mrs Eunice Murray told reporters that Marilyn had not seemed suicidal to her.

Below: Coroner Theodore Curphey (center) with Dr Norman Farberow on the left and Dr Robert Litman on the right, announce the findings of the psychiatric suicide team and the autopsy test on Marilyn to the Press. Her death is officially ruled as a "Probable Suicide".

Chronology

1926

1 Jun Marilyn is born Norma Jeane Mortensen in Los Angeles, California

13 Jun The new baby is left with the neighboring Bolender family after her mother returns to work

Dec At her christening, the baby is named Norma Jeane - but she spells her second name with and without the "e" throughout her childhood

1927

July The toddler Norma is nearly suffocated by her grandmother, Della Monroe, who is later admitted to the Metropolitan State Hospital in Norwalk, LA County

23 Aug Della dies of a heart attack in hospital

1933

Jun Norma Jeane leaves the Bolenders to live with her mother, Gladys, in North Hollywood

Aug Gladys obtains a mortgage and they move into a house on Arbol Street, sharing it with an English couple

Oct Gladys hears that her grandfather, Tilford Hogan, has committed suicide

1934

Jan Gladys is admitted to a rest home in Santa Monica, having suffered a mental breakdown

1935

Jan Gladys is committed to the Metropolitan State Hospital in Norwalk, LA County, with a diagnosis of paranoid schizophrenia

Apr Gladys's estate is assessed as she is no longer able to manage her affairs

1 Jun Grace McKee becomes responsible for liquidating Gladys's estate

13 Sept Norma Jeane is placed in the Los Angeles Orphans Home Society

1936

26 Feb Papers are legally filed to allow Grace to become Norma Jeane's legal guardian

1937

Spring Grace becomes Norma Jeane's legal guardian

26 Jun Norma Jeane leaves the orphanage and lives with Grace and her new husband

Nov Norma Jeane goes to live with Ida Martin, a distant relative in Compton, LA

1938

Aug Norma Jeane goes to live with Anna Lower, Grace's aunt

1941

Dec Norma Jeane begins dating Jim Dougherty

1942

19 Jun Norma Jeane marries Jim Dougherty and the newlyweds move into an apartment

1943

Spring Jim and Norma Jeane move back to his parents' home, to look after it while they are away

Fall The young couple move into their own apartment again

Jim Dougherty is called up and joins the Merchant Marines - he is sent first as an instructor to Catalina Island

1944

Spring Jim is posted to a ship in the South Pacific

Apr Marilyn returns to her mother-in-law's home and starts work at Radio Plane Munitions Factory in Burbank, California

1945

26 Jun At Radio Plane, Marilyn is photographed by David Conover for a feature in *Yank* magazine

2 Aug Marilyn is taken on by the Blue Book Agency

1946

26 Apr First appearance of Norma Jeane on the cover of a national magazine, *Family Circle*

Jun Norma Jeane dyes her brunette hair blonde

Jul Harry Lipton of National Concert Artists Corporation becomes Norma Jeane's agent

16 Jul Norma Jeane has her first interview with Ben Lyon at Twentieth Century Fox

19 Jul At a screen test for Twentieth Century Fox, Norma Jeane comes over very well

29 Jul First mention of Norma Jeane (as Jean Norman) in a Hollywood gossip column

26 Aug The aspiring actress signs her first studio contract, with Twentieth Century Fox, and changes her name to Marilyn Monroe

Sept While in Las Vegas to obtain her divorce, Norma Jeane spends time in Las Vegas General Hospital, first with an acute mouth infection after her wisdom teeth are removed, and then with measles

13 Sept Norma Jeane is granted a divorce from Jim Dougherty in Las Vegas, Nevada

1947

Summer Filming of *Dangerous Years*, with Marilyn's first speaking role

Although Marilyn's first movie role is in *Scudda Hoo, Scudda Hay*, most of her part is later cut

Summer Filming of *Dangerous Years* with Marilyn's first speaking part

26 Jul Marilyn is told that her contract with Twentieth Century Fox is not to be renewed

25 Aug Marilyn's contract with Twentieth Century Fox runs out

4 Dec Marilyn signs a management contract with Lucille Ryman and John Carroll

7 Dec Release of *Dangerous Years*

1948

Feb Marilyn meets Joe Schenck at a Hollywood party

20 Feb Marilyn is crowned Miss California Artichoke Queen

14 Apr *Scudda Hoo, Scudda Hay* is released

9 Mar Marilyn signs a six-month contract with Columbia

Vocal coach Fred Karger works with Marilyn on her songs for *Ladies of the Chorus*, but her devotion to him is not reciprocated

Apr Marilyn meets Natasha Lytess, head drama coach at Columbia, who later becomes her personal drama coach for some years

Filming of *Ladies of the Chorus*

9 Sept Marilyn's contract with Columbia is not renewed

22 Oct Release of *Ladies of the Chorus*

31 Dec Marilyn meets agent Johnny Hyde from the William Morris Agency at Sam Spiegel's New Year party

1949

Feb Marilyn films a part in *Love Happy*, and is mentioned in Louella Parsons' gossip column

27 May Marilyn poses nude for the famous calendar photograph by Tom Kelley, which is published anonymously

24 Jul Earl Wilson first interviews Marilyn

15 Aug Start of shooting on *A Ticket to Tomahawk*

Johnny Hyde becomes Marilyn's agent

Marilyn films a small uncredited part in *Right Cross*

Oct MGM give Marilyn a contract for a role in *The Asphalt Jungle*

10 Oct *Life* magazine shows pictures of Marilyn in a feature on Hollywood's aspiring stars

1950

5 Jan Marilyn begins shooting *The Fireball*

8 Apr Release of *Love Happy*

27 Mar Marilyn lands the part of a starlet in *All About Eve*

19 May Release of *A Ticket to Tomahawk*

23 May World première of *The Asphalt Jungle* at Grauman's Egyptian Theater

14 Oct Release of *All About Eve*

9 Nov Release of *The Fireball*

15 Nov Release of *Right Cross*

10 Dec Marilyn signs a contract with Twentieth Century Fox

18 Dec Johnny Hyde dies of a heart attack

Dec Marilyn has minor plastic surgery, possibly to remove a small lump from her nose

Dec	Marilyn appears in *As Young As You Feel* for Fox
Dec	Arthur Miller and Marilyn meet for the first time on the set of *As Young As You Feel* at Twentieth Century Fox

1951

Mar	After catching the attention of Spyros Skouras, president of Fox, Marilyn secures the renewal of her contract
29 Mar	Marilyn is a presenter at the 1951 Academy Awards ceremony
18 Apr	Starts shooting *The Love Nest* for Fox
11 May	The six-month contract with Fox is converted to a seven-year contract
	Release of *Hometown Story*
	Films a part in *Let's Make it Legal* for Fox
2 Aug	Release of *As Young As You Feel*
21 Aug	Fox agrees to loan Marilyn to RKO, to appear in *Clash by Night*
8 Sept	The first full-length feature on Marilyn appears in Colliers magazine
Fall	Marilyn tries to contact C. Stanley Gifford, the man she believed was her father, but he refuses to see her
	Marilyn enrols to study acting with coach Michael Chekov
	Filming of *Clash by Night*
	Filming of *Don't Bother to Knock*
10 Oct	Release of *Love Nest*
23 Oct	Marilyn appears on the cover of *Look* magazine for the first time
6 Nov	Release of *Let's Make It Legal*
15 Nov	*Quick* magazine has a feature on Marilyn as its cover story, designating her "The New Jean Harlow"
Dec	*Focus* magazine has a cover story on Marilyn, comparing her favorably with Lana Turner, Betty Grable and Rita Hayworth

1952

26 Feb	Marilyn begins filming *Monkey Business*
13 Mar	After the Press discover Marilyn's nude calendar picture, she admits publicly that she is the model
15 Mar	Joe DiMaggio and Marilyn meet for the first time
7 Apr	Marilyn features on her first *Life* magazine cover
28 Apr	Marilyn's appendix is removed at the Cedars of Lebanon hospital
3 May	Studio publicity about Marilyn had presented her as an orphan, but after it is discovered that

	her mother is still alive, she releases a short statement to the Press
1 Jun	Marilyn learns she has the part of Lorelei in *Gentlemen Prefer Blondes*
Jun	Start of filming of *Niagara*
18 Jun	Release of *Clash By Night*
12 Jul	General release of *We're Not Married*
18 Jul	Release of *Don't Bother to Knock*
Aug	New York première of *Don't Bother to Knock*

31 Aug Marilyn's first live radio show is broadcast, in which she reads a role in a one-act play

1 Sept The U.S. Army photographs Marilyn to use in a recruitment drive, but the pictures are withdrawn after the photographer shoots from a balcony, revealing too much of the Monroe cleavage

2 Sept At the Miss America beauty pageant, Marilyn is a Grand Marshal

5 Sept General release of *Monkey Business*

16 Oct Release of *O Henry's Full House*

26 Oct Marilyn is heard on ventriloquist Edgar Bergen's radio show

17 Nov Filming begins on *Gentlemen Prefer Blondes*

22 Nov An article titled "The Truth about Me" appears in The American Weekly, with Marilyn's name as the by-line

1953

Jan The famous nude picture of Marilyn is republished as "Miss Golden Dreams" on the January page of a new calendar

21 Jan *Niagara* is released

9 Feb Gladys Baker is transferred to Rockhaven Sanatorium at Marilyn's expense

6 Mar Filming on *Gentlemen Prefer Blondes* is completed

9 Mar Scandal follows Marilyn's appearance at the *Photoplay* magazine awards in the tissue-thin gold lamé gown from *Gentlemen Prefer Blondes*

Mar *Photoplay* features an article by Jim Dougherty, "Marilyn Monroe Was My Wife"

Apr Start of filming on *How to Marry a Millionaire*

May Marilyn is featured on the cover of *Cosmopolitan* magazine

26 Jun Marilyn and Jane Russell both leave their prints outside Grauman's Chinese Theater

15 Jul Release of *Gentlemen Prefer Blondes*

Aug Filming of *River of No Return* in Canada

20 Aug During filming, Marilyn slips and damages her leg

Aug Official première of *Gentlemen Prefer Blondes* at Grauman's Chinese Theater

13 Sept Marilyn's first television appearance on *The Jack Benny Show*

Oct Marilyn signs a recording contract with RCA

10 Oct Marilyn accompanies Joe DiMaggio to visit his family in San Francisco

4 Nov Première of *How to Marry a Millionaire* in Los Angeles

Dec The famous nude calendar shot appears in the first issue of *Playboy* magazine, as the first Sweetheart of the Month, and a clothed Marilyn also appears on the cover

15 Dec Marilyn fails to report on the first day of rehearsals of *The Girl in Pink Tights*

1954

4 Jan Fox suspends Marilyn for failing to appear for filming

14 Jan Marilyn marries baseball player Joe DiMaggio at San Francisco City Hall

2 Feb The couple arrive in Tokyo for their honeymoon

16 Feb During their honeymoon, Marilyn takes time to entertain the troops in Korea

5 Mar Marilyn arrives back in Los Angeles

14 Mar Marilyn is voted Best New Actress of 1953 by *Photoplay* magazine

31 Mar Charles Feldman at Famous Artists Agency officially becomes Marilyn's agent

14 Apr After the lifting of her suspension, Marilyn returns to the studio

30 Apr Release of *River of No Return*

28 May Starts filming *There's No Business Like Show Business*

7 Jul A representative of the armed forces presents Marilyn with a trophy and plaque for morale-building activities

10 Aug Filming begins on *The Seven Year Itch*

9 Sept Marilyn arrives in New York for location filming on *The Seven Year Itch*

10 Sept Milton Greene photographs Marilyn as a ballerina

16 Sept The famous skirt-blowing sequence for *The Seven Year Itch* is filmed on the streets of New York

5 Oct Marilyn and Joe DiMaggio officially separate

27 Oct A divorce from DiMaggio is granted, but not finalized for one year

4 Nov Shooting finishes on *The Seven Year Itch*

5 Nov Joe DiMaggio and Frank Sinatra carry out the "Wrong Door" raid, attempting to find Marilyn

6 Nov Marilyn is honored at a Hollywood party at Romanoff's

7 Nov Marilyn enters the Cedars of Lebanon Hospital to undergo surgery for endometriosis

Dec Leaving Hollywood, Marilyn heads for New York

16 Dec Release of *There's No Business Like Show Business*

31 Dec Marilyn Monroe Productions is officially formed

1955

7 Jan Milton Greene and Marilyn hold a Press conference to announce the creation of Marilyn Monroe Productions

10 Jan Marilyn returns briefly to Hollywood to film one scene of additional dialogue for *The Seven Year Itch*

15 Jan Fox suspends Marilyn again

Feb Marilyn begins to study under Lee Strasberg, founder of the Actors Studio in New York

9 Mar At the première of East of Eden, Marilyn acts as an usherette in aid of the Actors Studio

30 Mar At the opening of the Ringling Brothers Barnum & Bailey Circus, Marilyn appears riding a pink elephant in aid of the New York Arthritis & Rheumatism Foundation

8 Apr Edward R. Murrow interviews Marilyn live on *Person to Person*

Summer Marilyn briefly dates Marlon Brando, and when they split up they remain friends

1 Jun World première of *The Seven Year Itch*

26 Jul Breaking her agency contract with Famous Artists, Marilyn signs with MCA

29 Sept Marilyn attends the opening night of Arthur Miller's play, *A View from the Bridge*, at New York's Coronet Theater

31 Oct The divorce from Joe DiMaggio is finalized

31 Dec Marilyn signs a new four-picture, seven-year contract with Fox

1956

4 Jan Twentieth Century Fox announce that they and Marilyn have come to terms, and that she will be returning to Hollywood

9 Feb At a Press conference in New York, Laurence Olivier announces their joint project, *The Prince and the Showgirl*

17 Feb Marilyn performs at the Actors' Studio, New York

23 Feb Norma Jeane legally changes her name to Marilyn Monroe

25 Feb Marilyn returns to Hollywood after her one-year exile in New York

3 Mar Filming begins on *Bus Stop*

12 Apr Suffering from bronchitis, Marilyn spends four days in St Vincent Hospital, Los Angeles

14 May *Time* magazine features Marilyn on the cover for the first and only time in her lifetime

11 Jun A divorce is granted to playwright Arthur Miller

29 Jun Marilyn marries Miller in a civil ceremony

1 Jul Marilyn and Miller have a Jewish wedding ceremony

14 Jul The Millers fly to London

7 Aug *The Prince and the Showgirl* starts filming in England

31 Aug Release of *Bus Stop*

Sept Marilyn becomes pregnant, but loses the baby within a few weeks

29 Oct Marilyn is presented to Queen Elizabeth II at the Royal Command Performance of *The Battle of the River Plate* in London

17 Nov Filming completed on *The Prince and the Showgirl*

20 Nov The Millers return to America

18 Dec Marilyn does a radio show broadcast from the Waldorf-Astoria

1957

18 Feb Miller is indicted by a federal grand jury on two counts of contempt of Congress

27 Feb Frank Sinatra testifies at an investigation into the "Wrong Door" raid carried out by Joe DiMaggio in 1954

1 Mar At a first hearing, Miller pleads not guilty

11 Apr A statement is released, accusing Greene of mismanaging Marilyn Monroe Productions

14 May After being called to Washington, Arthur Miller is put on trial for contempt of Congress; Marilyn accompanies him but stays out of sight

13 Jun Première of *The Prince and the Showgirl*

1 Aug Marilyn is rushed to Doctors Hospital, New York, with severe abdominal pain, which turns out to be an ectopic pregnancy that has to be terminated

10 Aug Marilyn leaves hospital under a barrage of Press attention

1958

28 Jan Marilyn attends the annual March of Dimes fashion show at the Waldorf-Astoria, New York

4 Apr After prevaricating, Marilyn signs the contract for *Some Like It Hot*

7 Jul Marilyn returns to Hollywood to prepare for filming

4 Aug Filming begins on *Some Like It Hot*

Oct Marilyn becomes pregnant again

6 Nov Filming on *Some Like It Hot* is completed

16 Dec Marilyn miscarries the baby, and is taken to Polyclinic Hospital in New York

1959

29 Mar Première of *Some Like It Hot* at Loew's Capitol Theater on Broadway

Jun Marilyn receives the David Di Donatello statuette from Italy for her performance in *The Prince and the Showgirl*

23 Jun Corrective gynecological surgery is carried out on Marilyn at the Lennox Hill Hospital, New York, to try to cure her chronic endometriosis

18 Sept The Russian premier, Nikita Khrushchev, meets Marilyn at a luncheon in his honor at the Twentieth Century Fox studios in Hollywood

14 Oct Although Marilyn is due to begin rehearsing in New York for *The Billionaire* - later released as *Let's Make Love* - she fails to show

9 Nov Marilyn officially begins work on *Let's Make Love*

1960

25 Jan The first part of one of Marilyn's musical numbers in *Let's Make Love* is finally filmed

8 Mar Marilyn receives a Golden Globe award for Best Actress in a Comedy, for *Some Like It Hot*

Yves Montand and Marilyn have a brief affair during the filming of *Let's Make Love*

Jun Psychoanalyst Ralph Greenson begins seeing Marilyn on a daily basis

18 Jul Filming begins on *The Misfits*

27 Aug Marilyn is admitted to Westside Hospital in Los Angeles suffering from exhaustion

5 Sept Marilyn returns to Nevada to finish location filming on *The Misfits*

8 Sept Release of *Let's Make Love*

4 Nov Shooting finishes on *The Misfits*

Nov Yves Montand sees Marilyn briefly in New York, before returning to his wife in France

11 Nov Arthur Miller and Marilyn officially separate

16 Nov Clark Gable dies of a heart attack

1961

20 Jan A divorce from Arthur Miller is granted in Juarez, Mexico

31 Jan Première of *The Misfits*

7 Feb Marilyn enters the Payne-Whitney Clinic in New York under the name Faye Miller

11 Feb After three days, Joe DiMaggio arranges for Marilyn to be transferred to the Neurological Institute at Columbia-Presbyterian Hospital

5 Mar Marilyn leaves the Columbia-Presbyterian Hospital

Mar Margaret Parton interviews Marilyn for the *Ladies Home Journal*, but the interview is never published as it is deemed "too sympathetic" by the editor

May Again Marilyn enters the Cedars of Lebanon Hospital for a minor operation

Summer Frank Sinatra and Marilyn have a brief affair

28 June Marilyn enters Polyclinic Hospital in New York to have her gall bladder removed

11 Jul Marilyn leaves hospital

8 Aug Finally giving up on New York, Marilyn returns to Hollywood

Oct	Robert Kennedy and Marilyn begin an affair, after meeting at Peter Lawford's beach house
19 Nov	Marilyn attends a dinner at Peter Lawford's beach house, President John Kennedy is also present

1962

Feb	Marilyn buys a new home in Brentwood, California
21 Feb	With her housekeeper, Marilyn flies to Mexico to buy furniture and artefacts for her new home
2 Mar	Marilyn returns from Mexico
5 Mar	At the Golden Globe Awards, Marilyn is presented with a statuette as the World's Favorite Female Star
10 Apr	Marilyn attends costume and makeup tests for *Something's Got To Give*
23 Apr	Filming begins on *Something's Got To Give*
19 May	Marilyn sings "Happy Birthday" at a gala birthday party for President John Kennedy at Madison Square Garden
28 May	During filming, Marilyn is photographed swimming nude in a pool
1 Jun	Marilyn's last public appearance
8 Jun	Marilyn is fired from *Something's Got To Give* for persistent absenteeism
23 Jun	First *Vogue* photo session with Bert Stein
28 Jun	Negotiations with Fox begin about resuming work on *Something's Got To Give*
29 Jun	Start of a three-day photo session, with George Barris shooting Marilyn for *Cosmopolitan*
4 Jul	Richard Meryman begins an extensive interview with Marilyn, which turns out to be her last
12 Jul	Marilyn meets the studio chiefs at Fox
20 Jul	Marilyn enters the Cedars of Lebanon Hospital for an operation to cure her endometriosis
28 Jul	Marilyn spends the weekend at Cal-Neva Lodge
1 Aug	Fox revises Marilyn's contract, offering double her previous salary and agreeing to restart shooting on *Something's Got To Give*
3 Aug	Marilyn appears on the cover of *Life* magazine for the last time before her death
4 Aug	Dr Ralph Greenson spends six hours with Marilyn
5 Aug	Police are called after Marilyn is found dead in her Brentwood home
8 Aug	Marilyn's funeral, at Westwood Memorial Park, in Los Angeles, California

1995

1 Jun	A 32¢ commemorative postage stamp featuring Marilyn is issued in the US Legends of Hollywood series
Oct	Marilyn is voted UK's *Empire* magazine Sexiest Female Movie Star of All Time

1997

Oct	Marilyn is listed No.8 in the UK's *Empire* magazine The Top 100 Movie Stars of All Time

1998

Fall	Marilyn is voted *Playboy* magazine's Sexiest Female Star of the Twentieth Century

1999

Oct	At a Christie's auction of Marilyn memorabilia, the gown in which Marilyn sang "Happy Birthday" to John Kennedy is sold for over $1 million
Dec	*Playboy* magazine names Marilyn as Number One Sex Star of the Twentieth Century

Clark Gable
"Everything Marilyn does is different from any other woman, strange and exciting, from the way she talks to the way she uses that magnificent torso."

Billy Wilder
"She is a very great actress. Better Marilyn late than most of the others on time."

Barbara Stanwyck
"She wasn't disciplined, and she was often late but there was a sort of magic about her which we all recognized at once."

Edward Wagenknecht
"Marilyn played the best game with the worst hand of anybody I know."

Sam Shaw
"Everybody knows about her insecurities, but not everybody knows what fun she was, that she never complained about the ordinary things of life, that she never had a bad word to say about anyone, and that she had a wonderful spontaneous sense of humor."

Sammy Davis Jr.
"Still she hangs like a bat in the heads of men who have met her, and none of us will ever forget her."

Joe DiMaggio
"If it hadn't been for her friends she might still be alive."

Marilyn on Marilyn

"I'm not interested in money, I just want to be wonderful."

"I've been on a calendar, but never on time."

"Hollywood's a place where they'll pay you a thousand dollars for a kiss,
and fifty cents for your soul. I know, because I turned down the first offer
often enough and held out for the fifty."

"A sex-symbol becomes a thing, I just hate being a thing.
But if I'm going to be a symbol of something, I'd rather have it sex than some
of the other things we've got symbols of."

"If I had observed all the rules, I'd never have gotten anywhere."

"Some people have been unkind. If I say I want to grow as an actress,
they look at my figure. If I say I want to develop, to learn my craft, they laugh.
Somehow they don't expect me to be serious about my work."

"Dogs never bite me. Just humans."

Acknowlegements

All photographs in this book are reproduced
by kind permsission of
Corbis except those listed below.

Photographs on the following pages are reprodcued
by kind permission of
the Associated Newspapers Archive:
9, 183, 184, 185, 220, 221 (top and bottom),
222, 223, 224, 225 (top), 226, 227, 228, 229 (top and bottom), 230-1,
237 (bottom), 238 (top and bottom), 239, 240, 241, 242, 243, 244, 245,
246-7, 248, 250-1, 374, 375, 376 and 382

Robert Landau/Corbis: 87 bottom left
Jerry Ohlinger/Corbis: 115 top

Every effort has been made to ensure that the copyright details shown are correct,
but if there are any inaccuracies, please contact the publisher.

Bibliography

Marilyn Monroe   Barbara Leaming (Orion, London, 2002)

The Marilyn Encyclopedia   Adam Victor
(The Overlook Press, New York, 2001)

Norma Jean   Fred Lawrence Guiles
(Mayflower, St Albans, 1977)

My Story   Marilyn Monroe
(Stein & Day, New York, 1974)

The Pocket Essential Marilyn Monroe   Paul Donnelley
(Pocket Essentials, Harpenden, 2000)

Goddess, The Secret Lives of Marilyn Monroe   Anthony Summers
(Gollanz, London, 1985)

DiMaggio Setting the Record Straight   Morris Engleberg, Marv Schneider
(MBI, St Paul, 2003)

Blonde Heat   Richard Buskin
(Billboard Books, New York, 2001)

The Assassination of Marilyn Monroe   Donald H. Wolfe
(Time Warner Paperbacks, London 1998)

On Sunset Boulevard, The Life and Times of Billy Wilder   Ed Sikov
(Hyperion, New York, 1998)